THE
QUICK AFTER-WORK
ITALIAN
❖ Cookbook ❖

This edition published 1995
by BCA by arrangement with
Judy Piatkus (Publishers) Ltd

CN 8983

Designed by Paul Saunders
Illustrations by Madeleine David

Cover photograph by James Murphy shows
Pizza with Tomatoes and Garlic (page 65)

Data capture by Selwood Systems, Midsomer Norton, Avon
Printed and bound in Great Britain by
Butler & Tanner Ltd, Frome and London

THE
QUICK AFTER-WORK
ITALIAN
❖ *Cookbook* ❖

HILAIRE WALDEN

BCA

LONDON   NEW YORK   SYDNEY   TORONTO

Contents

Introduction

ITALIANS have an inherent love of good food and although most of them now have less time to spend in the kitchen this means that even the meals that are prepared quickly are prepared with care and attention. Italians shop with knowledge and discrimination, selecting only top quality, natural produce that bursts with abundant flavour. These tasty ingredients are combined with flair and cooked with skill to make dishes that, according to style, ooze or explode with exuberant flavour – zesty lemon, fragrant basil or piquant capers combined with salty anchovies.

Even with changing life styles and food preferences, Italian cooks tend to steer away from creativity for creativity's sake, preferring instead to stay with tradition and the local dishes of their region, town or village. This does not mean that they are blind to change, but that innovations are composed with care and sensitivity, making the most sympathetic use of the best, seasonal if appropriate, ingredients. You will therefore find that the recipes in this book conform to the true characteristic style that has made Italian food so popular.

You will also find that not only can all the recipes be prepared very quickly with the minimum of effort, but that they cook quickly as well. All the dishes will be ready to eat in under 30 minutes and many in less time than that.

To make recipe preparation and cooking as straightforward and as quick as possible, it pays to get into the habit of following just a few simple steps.

When you are planning to serve more than one dish, choose recipes whose preparation and cooking will fit easily together. For example, team a first course that has to be prepared and cooked at the last minute with a main one that can be prepared ahead of time and then left to cook. Conversely, choose a simple first course that requires little or no cooking to precede a main one that calls for more attention. Accompany such a main course with a plain or simply cooked vegetable. If you are using the oven for one dish, choose another that can also be baked.

Before starting to prepare a meal, check that you have all the ingredients you will need. Remove them from the refrigerator, if necessary, so that they can at least start to reach room temperature; 'fridge-cold' ingredients take longer to cook. Then read through the entire recipe – this won't take long and you could well find that you can remember all of it so that you do not have to waste time breaking off in the middle of cooking to find out what to do next. You will also know when to preheat the grill or bring water to the boil in advance, which ingredients to prepare first and which can be prepared while others are cooking.

Cooking times vary according to the ingredients that are being used. For example, young vegetables cook more speedily than old ones and small or thin pieces of food obviously cook more quickly than large or fat ones. Diced butter melts more rapidly, and evenly, than a single piece. The temperature of the equipment when you start to cook, as well as that of the ingredients, will also affect the cooking time.

Please regard my recipes as guides and adapt them if you like. The measurements suited my taste and that of my friends when I tested the recipes, but the flavours of fresh ingredients are not constant, branded goods vary and everyone has their personal preferences. So do try to get into the habit of tasting while you are preparing a dish and before you serve it – this is the simplest of skills to learn from good cooks.

Ingredients

Italians respect and expect quality and, thank goodness, we can now buy many similar ingredients. For example sun-dried tomatoes, once a rarity, are easily available today; many shops sell pesto and savoury pastes like black olive; salt-packed capers can be found without too much trouble. I live in a hamlet near a small village in a very pastoral location in Dorset, yet bought everything I needed for this book in the vicinity. If you can't find what you want in a local supermarket try delicatessens or one of the mail order companies that specialises in unusual ingredients.

The following items are well worth keeping in your store cupboard or buying regularly as they provide ammunition for inspiration in creating quick, tasty dishes.

ANCHOVIES

I prefer salted anchovies rather than fillets canned in oil as they have a superior flavour and dissolve more readily when heated. Although they must be carefully boned, washed and dried before they can be used, you can do this when you have time and keep the resulting fillets, covered with olive oil, in a jar.

BALSAMIC VINEGAR

Although it has recently become fashionable, balsamic vinegar has in fact been made for hundreds of years. Its unique, rich, sweet, nutty taste is due to the special way it is made. Grapes are thickened by cooking down, then fermented over a period of years in a succession of barrels made from different woods. The vinegar should be at least four or five years old when it is sold, but may be anything up to 40 years or more. Because they evaporate and concentrate as they mature, older vinegars become thicker and the flavour richer. They also become progressively more expensive; even young balsamic vinegars are not cheap.

Balsamic vinegar should be treated more like a condiment or seasoning than a standard vinegar; just a few drops of even a cheaper one will add a unique, rich sweet-sour flavour to salad dressings and sauces (add it towards the end of cooking as overheating spoils the flavour). Try sprinkling a few drops over grilled meats and poultry to give them a quick lift.

BREADS

The range and quality of breads available in supermarkets, bakers and grocers has improved enormously in recent years and it is now possible to buy very good, firm-textured, well-flavoured Italian breads such as ciabatta and foccacia. If you cannot find these breads, use any other similar bread such as French country bread (*pain de campagne*).

CAPERS

When the flavour and quality of capers is important to the overall quality of a dish, I always use ones that have been packed in salt, rather than those that have been preserved in brine. Rinse well before use to remove all the salt.

CHEESES

Italy has one of the world's finest selections of quality, original cheeses.

Dolcelatte

A smooth, blue-veined, quite mild factory-produced cheese, it is made by the firm of Galbani and the name is a registered trade mark.

Gorgonzola

This has the texture of ripe brie and is marbled with blue-green veins which contrast beautifully with the creaminess of the cheese. Depending on the variety, gorgonzola can be quite mild and creamy tasting, or fairly piquant, but it should never be strong or taste of ammonia.

Mascarpone

A voluptuous, velvety fresh cheese with a mild, slightly sweet taste, mascarpone is sold in tubs in the chiller cabinets of supermarkets. It should be used soon after purchase or the flavour will deteriorate.

Mozzarella

Genuine mozzarella is made from the milk of water buffaloes and has a more pronounced, yet delicate, fresher and more fragrant, flavour than the more common cows' milk version. It is also more compact, fairly elastic, whiter and will 'ooze' tears of whey when cut. It is not only made in Italy and much of the mozzarella on sale has a rubbery texture and virtually no taste.

Parmesan

True *Parmigiano Reggiano* can only be made between May and November, from cows' milk from designated provinces. Its manufacture is governed by strict laws and the name appears on the cheese. As well as being an essential cheese for Italian cooking, Parmesan can be served in chunks or slices for eating with bread or salads or with fruits such as pears as a dessert. Never buy cardboard tubs of ready grated Parmesan – the taste and texture are far removed from those of the true product. Instead, buy it by the piece and grate or slice it as needed.

Pecorino

This hard cheese is made all over the south of Italy from sheep's milk and can vary in flavour and piquancy. Pecorino Romano is stronger and drier than pecorino. Pecorino is a good cheese for grating or cutting into slivers, or serving at table. Like Parmesan, it goes well with pears.

Ricotta

Made from the whey from other cheeses, ricotta should be eaten very fresh when it has a delicate, clean, fresh taste; it quite quickly begins to taste rancid.

GARLIC

It is impossible to do much authentic Italian cooking without using garlic. If you are a garlic fan and tend to use it generously, remember that the quick cooking times in this book mean that the flavour will be at its most pronounced (it mellows with long, slow cooking). For a milder taste, use whole or halved cloves rather than chopped or crushed ones. When cooking dishes in oil, you can fry the garlic first to add flavour, then remove it before putting in other ingredients.

I prefer to buy loose bulbs rather than those packed in cardboard boxes as I find they keep better. It is also easier to check that the individual cloves are plump and firm. Keep garlic in a cool, dry, airy place. If any green shoots start to appear, cut the clove lengthways before using it and discard the shoots as they taste bitter.

HERBS

With the exception of bunches of dried oregano from southern Italy and Greece, fresh herbs have a far superior taste to dried ones and as they are now so readily available in supermarkets, markets and grocers there is no reason for not using them. Some herbs are even sold in pots. It is also very easy to grow basic herbs such as parsley and chives, even if you do not have a garden – a window box or pots on a sunny windowsill will suffice.

If you really cannot get fresh herbs, choose freeze-dried or frozen ones, both of which are sold in supermarkets.

The flavour and pungency of any fresh herb will vary with its growing conditions and time of year. Therefore, quantities given in recipes can only be guides and it is worth getting into the habit of tasting herbs before using them in order to judge their flavour and strength and adjust amounts. Don't forget to taste the dish at the end of cooking so that you can fine-tune the flavour if necessary.

Keep freshly cut herbs in 'stay fresh' bags, available from health food stores and some supermarkets. Keep herbs sold in pots on a sunny window sill. If you have more herbs than you need, freeze them in small quantities. I have never dried them entirely to my satisfaction in a microwave oven.

I use the flat-leaved, or Continental, parsley.

OLIVE OIL

A burgeoning range of olive oils of different styles and varying qualities is now available, and choice is a matter of personal preference and the use to which the oil is to be put.

In descending order of quality, purity, intensity of flavour and price, the grades in which olive oils are sold are:

Extra virgin oil

This results from the first pressing of the olives, and has the lowest acidity and, therefore, the most rounded flavour. Commercially produced extra virgin oils are blended from different oils and always taste the same. Ones produced by estates, farms and village co-operatives have their own individual characters and, as they are unblended, will vary from year to year like the best producer-bottled wines.

Virgin oil

This comes from the second pressing of the olives.

Olive oil

This used to be called pure olive oil and is a blend of virgin olive oil and refined oils obtained by chemical extraction.

The colour of an oil is no indication of quality – a rich dark green does not necessarily mean it is superior – but it is an indication of the amount of flavour it contains.

The taste, texture and colour of the oils vary according to the type of olives used, where they have grown and ripened, their degree of ripeness when picked and how they have been handled and pressed. Tuscan oils, for example, are peppery, grassy and green while Ligurian ones are golden, delicate and light. Buy small bottles of different types, preferably after tasting them – some specialist food shops will allow you to do this.

Different grades and varieties suit different purposes. I use light extra virgin oil for salad dressings or when only small quantities of oil are required and richer, more full-bodied ones for brushing on meats and poultry before grilling, tossing with pasta, trickling over firm-textured bread or toast or stirring into soups such as Pasta and Chick Pea Soup (see page 6). I use virgin oil for salads or more widely in cooking, and simple olive oil for cooking.

Store olive oils in a cool, dark place but preferably not in a refrigerator.

OLIVE PASTES

These are made with puréed olives – black or green – and olive oil and are usually flavoured with herbs, and sometimes garlic and anchovies.

I invariably have a jar of black olive paste in my store cupboard as it comes in very handy for spreading on crostini or pizza bases, using with crème fraîche to make an instant sauce for pasta and livening up salad dressings.

PANCETTA

Like bacon, pancetta is made from pork belly. Also like bacon, it has layers of fat and lean meat. Most pancetta is 'green' but some is smoked. There are two kinds of pancetta:

Pancetta stesa
This is left in its natural shape like bacon.

Pancetta arrotala
This is leaner and is flavoured with cloves and pepper and rolled.

Pancetta can be substituted for prosciutto in cooking. *Pancetta arrotala* is the best one to slice and serve at table, though, in this case, it is not a substitute for prosciutto.

PASTA

Quite a number of fresh pastas are available but fresh does not necessarily mean better than dried; in fact, some dried pastas are better than some fresh ones. However, good fresh pasta is deliciously light and almost melts in the mouth.

PESTO

Commercially produced bottled and fresh pesto sauces are available. They vary in taste, texture and quality; some are close to the home-made version, others are inferior. It is not difficult to make your own pesto, and it is worth making in summer when the flavour of basil is at its best. Using the traditional mortar and pestle produces pesto with the best flavour and texture but is a little laborious. The speed and ease of using a blender outweighs the loss in quality for many people, but for me the loss is too great.

If you make a lot of pesto pack it into small, airtight pots and refrigerate it (allow it to come to room temperature before using), or freeze it in ice-cube trays then keep the cubes in a plastic bag ready for individual ones to be thawed in the refrigerator as required. When I make pesto for freezing I prefer not to add the cheese until the sauce has thawed.

The classic way of using pesto is with trenette, the local Ligurian fettucine, but there are innumerable other uses: spooned on to sliced tomatoes; served with plainly cooked meats, poultry and fish; added to sauces, casseroles and soups; as a filling for rolled fish fillets; or mixed with soft cheese and slipped between the skin and flesh of a chicken or chicken portions.

PROSCIUTTO AND PARMA HAM

Prosciutto crudo, usually just labelled 'prosciutto', is cured and salted raw ham. It is produced throughout Italy and various styles and qualities are available. Parma ham can only be made around Parma, according to strict regulations, and is generally considered the best prosciutto although some *aficionados* prefer San Daniele.

STOCK

Many savoury recipes in this book do not need stock, but where it is called for I urge you to use the real thing not stock made from a cube. It is very easy to make perfectly adequate stock for quick cooking. Save chicken skin and bones and simmer them with an onion, carrot, perhaps a stick of celery, and a fresh bouquet garni for 20–40 minutes. If you do not need the stock within the next day or so, strain it and freeze it. Alternatively, freeze the skin and bones and make stock with them when you have time. Fish stock can be made in the same way, but is simmered for only 20 minutes.

Make vegetable stock by softening and lightly browning an onion in olive oil, then adding sliced leek, carrot and celery, some mushroom stalks and tomato skins and seeds and a bunch of fresh herbs. Cover with water and simmer for 20–40 minutes.

If you do not have any home-made stock, you can buy good chilled ones from supermarkets; you may like to keep a carton in the freezer.

SUN-DRIED TOMATOES

Buy these from a good shop or find a reputable brand of plump, well-flavoured tomatoes dried naturally under the hot Mediterranean sun. Price can be a good guide – cheap sun-dried tomatoes will not be genuine. Those preserved in olive oil are more expensive than dry ones. To have a supply of the dried variety ready for use, soak several at a time until they are plumped up, then drain them, dry them with paper towels and layer them in a jar with olive oil. Seal the jar and keep in a cool, dark place.

The oil from sun-dried tomatoes can be used in salad dressings or brushed on bread, toast and pizzas.

SUN-DRIED TOMATO PASTE

Because it is made from sun-dried tomatoes, this paste has a richer, more intense taste than tomato purée and I find it much better for boosting the flavour of tomato sauces. It also has many other uses: it adds depth and character to the flavour of all manner of sauces and salad dressings, it can be spread on breads and pizzas or it can be tossed with pasta.

TOMATOES

Tomatoes used to be universally flavourless and woolly but this dire situation is beginning to be redressed with supermarkets competing for the best tomatoes 'grown for flavour' (or words to that effect). It is also becoming easier to buy good Mediterranean ones from specialist greengrocers.

To skin and seed tomatoes, pour boiling water over them, leave for 1 minute, drain, then slip off the skins when cool enough to handle. Cut in half and scoop out the seeds.

Equipment

The amount and complexity of the equipment you will need for my recipes is minimal. I know that the occasions when I have little time for cooking are also those when I don't want to spend much time clearing and washing up. Although specialist items are not needed, here are a few utensils you may find helpful.

BLENDERS

I have a small blender as well as a normal sized one which I find too large for quite a number of tasks, especially if I am cooking for two people. I prefer to use the bigger blender instead of a food processor for puréeing soups and sauces as the results are better and a blender is considerably easier to wash up.

FRYING PANS

I advise having one large and one small heavy-based frying pan. Non-stick surfaces assist both cooking and washing up, but remember that they can be damaged if you are cooking over a very high heat, especially if the pan is dry.

KNIVES

Contrary to the often-stated opinion, it is not vital to have a set of expensive, really sharp knives. True, these do speed up chopping, slicing etc., but to gain most benefit from them you have to be able to use them proficiently. It is also true that a blunt knife is inefficient and cuts badly. Unless you do quite a lot of reasonably advanced and varied cooking, you can manage with a couple, or even just one, reasonably sharp knife (I know I have!).

HEATPROOF COLANDER
This is necessary for draining pasta quickly. It can also be used for steaming.

MANDOLINE SLICER/GRATER
This can be made of metal, wood or plastic, with adjustable steel blades for slicing and grating vegetables. I use my mandoline more than my food processor for these tasks as it is less prone to reducing foods like onions to a watery mass, takes up less room and is easier to wash up. A mandoline is also cheaper than a food processor.

MEZZALUNA
A mezzaluna is a two-handled, sickle-shaped blade that is useful for speedily chopping herbs, garlic, onions, etc.; if you are not very adept with a knife you will find it a boon. Mezzalunas are available in a range of sizes.

POTATO PEELER
Necessary for shaving Parmesan cheese.

LARGE SAUCEPAN
You will need this to cook pasta properly. As a general guide, you should have a saucepan that is large enough to hold 575 ml (1 pint) boiling water for each 115 g (4 oz) pasta.

Notes about the recipes

- I have given both metric and imperial measurements, but it is important to follow either one or the other. Don't mix metric and imperial.

- Unless otherwise stated I have used a moderate heat for both grilling and frying.

- Herbs are fresh unless otherwise stated.

First Courses & Snacks

TRADITIONALLY an evening meal in Italy was preceded by small,
tasty dishes known as *antipasti*. Recently, convention has been
overthrown as it has been discovered that these make ideal first courses
and snacks. A selection can also be served as a main course.
I find Italian soups very useful. They are speedy and uncomplicated
to prepare, the recipes are conveniently adaptable and the same soup
can do for a first course or be transformed into a light meal or snack
simply by adding croûtons or serving with bread and a salad.
You will find other recipes suitable for first courses and snacks in the
Vegetables and Salads chapter.

CAULIFLOWER AND PARMESAN SOUP

•

—— SERVES 4 ——

I F YOU have time to make croûtons, or have some already made, serve
them with the soup to add an appetising, contrasting crunch.

575ml (1 pint) vegetable or chicken
  stock
1 medium cauliflower
115ml (4fl oz) milk or single cream

2–3 tablespoons freshly grated
  Parmesan cheese
freshly grated nutmeg to taste
salt and freshly ground black pepper

1. Bring the stock to the boil. Divide the cauliflower into florets discarding tough parts of the stalk. Chop the slimmer parts of the stalks. Add the cauliflower florets and chopped stalks to the stock, cover and simmer until very tender.

2. Tip the soup into a food processor or blender, add the milk or cream and process until smooth, or leave a nubbly texture if you like.

3. Return the soup to the pan and stir in the Parmesan. Add nutmeg and seasoning and reheat gently; do not allow to boil.

To make croûtons: Cut day-old bread into cubes and cook until golden and crisp, either by frying them in olive oil or by tossing them with olive oil and baking them in a medium, slow or cooling (after the heat has been turned off) oven.

SPINACH SOUP

•

—— SERVES 4 ——

To MAKE the soup more creamy, reduce the quantity of milk slightly and either add a couple of tablespoons or so of mascarpone cheese when puréeing the spinach, or add a spoonful of the warmed mascarpone to each bowl as the soup is served. I like to add an interesting texture contrast by tossing warm croûtons (see opposite) with Parmesan cheese and serving them with the soup.

40–50g (1½–2oz) unsalted butter
1 fat leek, sliced
575g (1¼lb) fresh spinach
570ml (1 pint) vegetable or chicken
 stock

570ml (1 pint) milk
25g (1oz) freshly grated Parmesan
 cheese
freshly grated nutmeg to taste
salt and freshly ground black pepper

1. Heat the butter in a saucepan, add the leek and cook until softened. Stir in the spinach, cover and cook until it wilts. Pour in the stock, bring to the boil, then cover and simmer for 10 minutes.

2. Transfer the spinach and some of the stock to a blender and purée. Return to the pan, stir in the milk and add Parmesan, nutmeg and seasoning to taste. Reheat gently but do not allow to boil.

TOMATO AND BREAD SOUP

•

—— SERVES 4 ——

I FIND that 115–150g (4–5oz) of bread is about right, particularly in summer, but some people add more to make a more substantial soup. If preferred, you can leave out the breadcrumbs and instead put a slice of toasted bread in each soup bowl before pouring in the soup; leave to stand for a minute before serving with freshly grated Parmesan cheese.

3 tablespoons olive oil
1 onion, chopped
1 clove garlic
675g (1½lb) well-flavoured tomatoes
650ml (1¼ pints) vegetable stock

1–1½ tablespoons sun-dried tomato
   paste or tomato purée, or to taste
a large bunch of basil
115–150g (4–5oz) breadcrumbs
   made from firm day-old,
   preferably well-flavoured, bread
salt and freshly ground black pepper

1. Heat the oil in a saucepan, add the onion and cook gently until golden and softened.

2. Meanwhile, chop the garlic and quarter the tomatoes (peel them if you like). Add the garlic to the onion towards the end of cooking.

3. Stir the tomatoes, stock and sun-dried tomato paste or tomato purée into the pan and bring to the boil. Half-cover the pan and simmer for about 20 minutes.

4. Chop the basil and add most of it to the pan together with the breadcrumbs just before the end of cooking; reserve the remaining basil for garnish.

5. Season the soup and serve garnished with the remaining chopped basil.

POTATO AND ROCKET SOUP

•

—— SERVES 4 ——

Rocket adds its inimitable distinction to simple potato soup, transforming it into one with great character. It is a matter of personal preference whether or not you peel the potatoes. I always leave the skins on unless they are very thick because they add to the flavour and texture; it doesn't worry me if the skins of floury types of potatoes such as Maris Piper and King Edward come off during cooking – as they tend to.

2 tablespoons olive oil
2 cloves garlic, chopped
225 ($\frac{1}{2}$lb) potatoes
a handful of parsley leaves
1.5 litres (2$\frac{1}{2}$ pints) vegetable stock or
   water

115g (4oz) rocket
salt and freshly ground black pepper
extra virgin olive oil (optional) and
   freshly grated pecorino or
   Parmesan cheese to serve

1. Heat the oil in a large saucepan. Add the garlic and cook gently until fragrant.

2. Meanwhile, cut the potatoes into approximately 1.25cm ($\frac{1}{2}$ inch) pieces. Chop the parsley. Bring the stock or water to the boil.

3. Add the potatoes containing the garlic to the pan and stir for 2–3 minutes then stir in the rocket and parsley to mix well together. Pour in the stock or water, return to the boil and simmer, partially covered, until the potatoes are tender. Season.

4. Serve with a little extra virgin olive oil swirled through, if liked, and with a bowl of freshly grated pecorino or Parmesan to sprinkle over the soup.

PASTA AND CHICK PEA SOUP

•

—— SERVES 4 ——

THICK, warming and as garlicky as you like, this is a wonderful autumnal or winter snack or lunch. For more body, cut a slice of pancetta or smoked bacon, weighing about 50g (2oz) and about 5mm (¼ inch) thick, into dice and add to the soup. If you want to give extra character, swirl extra virgin olive oil into each bowlful; the oil can be varied according to where the olives were grown – for example, a Tuscan oil will contribute a full-bodied, peppery taste while one from further south will be more delicate.

2 tablespoons virgin olive oil
1 onion, chopped
1–3 cloves garlic, chopped
a small sprig of rosemary
2 large, well-flavoured tomatoes
1 × 400g (14oz) can chick peas

about 450ml (16fl oz) vegetable or chicken stock or water
150g (5oz) macaroni
salt and freshly ground black pepper
freshly grated Parmesan cheese to serve

1. Heat the oil in a saucepan, add the onion and garlic and fry until softened.

2. Remove the leaves from the rosemary sprig and chop them. Coarsely chop the tomatoes. Drain the chick peas and coarsely purée half of them with the tomatoes, rosemary and half the stock or water in a food processor or blender.

3. Stir the chick pea purée into the pan and bring to the boil. Cover and simmer gently for 5 minutes. Bring the remaining stock or water to the boil.

4. Add the boiling stock or water and the macaroni to the pan, stir, then cover and simmer until the macaroni is tender. Make sure there is plenty of liquid to allow the macaroni to swell and leave a soupy consistency; add more boiling stock or water if necessary.

5. Add the remaining chick peas to the pan, season and heat through for a few minutes. Serve with freshly grated Parmesan.

BLACK FIGS WITH PARMA HAM

•

—— SERVES 4 ——

ALTHOUGH melon and Parma ham have been eaten together for a long time, I think black figs make a more exciting accompaniment to the ham.

115ml (4fl oz) olive oil
2 tablespoons white wine vinegar
3 plump ripe black figs, quartered

12 thin slices of Parma ham
salt and freshly ground black pepper
mascarpone cheese to serve
(optional)

1. Whisk together the oil, vinegar and seasoning, then toss with the figs.

2. Lay out the ham slices and fold them lengthways, sides to middles. Place a fig quarter on one end of each piece of ham and roll up. Place with the loose ends down on serving plates. Serve with a little mascarpone cheese, if liked.

AUBERGINE AND MOZZARELLA ROLLS

•

As GRILLED slices of aubergine combine so readily with sliced mozzarella cheese I have devised a number of ways of varying the partnership. They are all equally good and, when I have more time and am cooking for a larger number, I sometimes prepare two or all of these recipes and serve a large aubergine and mozzarella cheese platter.

1 medium aubergine
about 115g (4oz) mozzarella cheese
about 8 basil leaves

virgin olive oil for brushing
salt and freshly ground black pepper

1. Preheat the grill. Cut the aubergine lengthways into about 8 slices. Season with pepper and brush with oil. Grill until tender and browned on one side but only lightly coloured on the other.

2. Meanwhile, cut the cheese into the same number of slices as the aubergine.

3. Lay a cheese slice on each aubergine slice, top with a basil leaf and roll up lengthways. Return to the grill, seam-side down, until the cheese softens. Sprinkle with salt and serve straight away.

——— VARIATIONS ———

1. For Aubergine and Mozzarella 'Sandwiches', thinly slice the aubergine, grill the slices and then sandwich them together with thinly sliced mozzarella. Add some finely chopped anchovy fillets, capers and parsley and grill until the cheese softens.

2. For Pizza-style Aubergine Slices, spread grilled aubergine slices with a little tomato sauce or passata. Cover with sliced mozzarella, top with some chopped anchovy fillet and return to the grill until the cheese is bubbling.

AUBERGINES WITH PESTO SAUCE

•

——— SERVES 4 ———

I LOVE the soft, silky texture and smoky taste of grilled aubergines, and the wonderful heady taste of pesto sauce, so it is hardly surprising that this dish is a long-standing favourite of mine. To reduce the already minimal work involved in preparing it you could use a good commercial pesto sauce.

2 aubergines

PESTO
2 cloves garlic
2 tablespoons pine nuts
about 15g ($\frac{1}{2}$oz) basil leaves
about 75ml (3fl oz) virgin olive oil,
    plus extra for brushing

3 tablespoons mixed freshly grated
    pecorino and Parmesan cheese,
    or all Parmesan cheese
freshly ground black pepper

1. Preheat the grill.

2. Meanwhile, cut the aubergines in half lengthways, then score deeply into the flesh in a diamond pattern. Take care not to pierce the skin. Brush with oil, then grill, cut-side up first, until tender and browned.

3. Meanwhile, make the pesto: Drop the garlic into a blender or food processor with the motor running, then add the pine nuts, basil leaves and oil. Mix until smooth and add the cheese. Mix very briefly. Season with black pepper.

4. Spread the pesto over the cut side of the aubergines and return to the grill until the pesto is just beginning to bubble.

GRILLED AUBERGINES, TOMATOES AND MOZZARELLA CHEESE

•

—— SERVES 4 ——

THE AROMA of this simple dish while it is cooking will give a boost to any jaded taste-buds, and its savoury taste will perk up any flagging appetite.

1 small aubergine weighing about
   200g (7oz)
3 tablespoons virgin olive oil
150g (5oz) mozzarella cheese
450g (1lb) firm but ripe well-
   flavoured tomatoes

finely grated zest of 1 lemon
salt and freshly ground black pepper
4 tablespoons torn basil leaves and
   warm firm bread to serve

1. Preheat the grill. Thinly slice the aubergine and brush very lightly with some of the oil. Lay the slices in a single layer on the grill rack and grill until golden on both sides.

2. Meanwhile, thinly slice the cheese and tomatoes. Whisk together the remaining oil, the lemon zest and seasoning.

3. Lay the aubergines, cheese and tomatoes in a single layer of slightly overlapping slices in a large, shallow, heatproof dish. Pour the dressing over.

4. Grill for 3–4 minutes until the cheese begins to melt. Sprinkle with the basil leaves and serve straight away with warm firm bread.

GRILLED RADICCHIO WITH GOAT'S CHEESE

•

—— SERVES 4 ——

THIS recipe uses goat's cheese but, if preferred, you could omit making a hollow in the radicchio halves and simply sprinkle the grilled radicchio with freshly grated Parmesan, which should begin to melt just from the heat of the leaves. Or you could sprinkle the grilled halves with grated fontina or mozzarella before returning them to the grill until the cheese melts over the radicchio.

2 heads of radicchio
4 tablespoons extra virgin olive oil
3–4 slices of fresh goat's cheese,
   about 6mm ($\frac{1}{4}$ inch) thick

leaves from 2–3 sprigs of thyme
salt and freshly ground black pepper

1. Preheat the grill. Cut the radicchio into halves lengthways and scoop out a few of the leaves from the centre. (You can either use these in a salad or eat them as they are.) Brush the radicchio with some of the oil. Season, using plenty of pepper. Grill until beginning to brown at the edges.

2. Put a slice of cheese in the hollow of each piece of radicchio, brush with more oil and sprinkle with the thyme leaves. Return to the grill until the cheese begins to bubble. Grind black pepper over the radicchio and serve.

SWEET AND SOUR BABY ONIONS

•

—— SERVES 4 ——

THE ONIONS used in Italy for preparing this dish are sold in bunches, like spring onions in Britain; indeed, I have made this recipe using the very fat spring onions that can be bought from Middle Eastern food shops. They take less time to cook and using them saves the fiddle of having to skin baby onions. Another way to overcome the peeling- and cooking-time problems is to use frozen peeled button onions available from large supermarkets; there is no need to thaw them.

350g (12oz) frozen peeled button
  onions
2 tablespoons olive oil
2 tablespoons balsamic vinegar

1 bay leaf, torn
a pinch of brown sugar
freshly ground black pepper

1. Simmer the onions in salted water for about 5 minutes. Drain well.

2. Heat the oil in a heavy frying pan large enough to hold the onions in a single layer, add the onions and fry, turning them occasionally, until browned.

3. Add the vinegar, bay leaf, sugar and pepper and continue to cook, turning the onions until they are coated with a slightly syrupy sauce.

4. Discard the bay leaf and serve warm.

ITALIAN STUFFED MUSHROOMS

•

—— SERVES 2 – 4 ——

THE FILLING can be flavoured with anchovy paste or chopped anchovy fillets (in which case, halve the cheese). If it is more convenient the mushrooms can be cooked under a moderate grill.

4 large open mushrooms or field
   mushrooms
1 small well-flavoured tomato,
   seeded and chopped
4 tablespoons freshly grated
   Parmesan cheese

25g (1oz) fresh breadcrumbs
1 egg, beaten
1 clove garlic, finely chopped
about 1 tablespoon chopped parsley
1 tablespoon virgin olive oil
salt and freshly ground black pepper

1. Preheat the oven to 220°C/425°F/Gas Mark 7. Oil a shallow baking dish.

2. Chop the mushroom stalks, then mix with the tomato, cheese, breadcrumbs, egg, garlic, parsley, 1 teaspoon of the oil and the seasoning.

3. Put the mushroom caps in the dish, open side up, fill with the breadcrumb mixture and trickle the remaining oil over them. Bake for about 15 minutes until the mushrooms are cooked to your liking and the tops are brown.

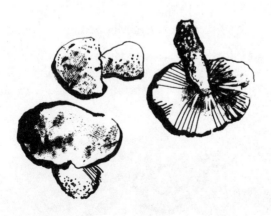

BAGNA CAUDA

•

—— SERVES 4 – 6 ——

*B*AGNA CAUDA, also spelled *bagna coâda*, is a rich, pungent, anchovy and garlic sauce or dip from Piedmont. It is served in very much the same way as a fondue, that is, in a small pot set over a spirit flame placed in the middle of the table. Raw or lightly cooked vegetables (traditionally, and in season, cardoons are the correct ones to offer) are served for dipping in the *bagna cauda*; the sauce is also good spooned over halved hard-boiled eggs. When there is only a small amount of sauce left, eggs are added to it and scrambled. Leftover *bagna cauda* (without the scrambled eggs) is good with pasta. The proportions of butter and oil can be altered to taste and cream is sometimes used to mute the pungency.

1 × 50g (2oz) can anchovy fillets in oil
4 plump cloves garlic, finely chopped
150ml (5fl oz) olive oil
75g (3oz) unsalted butter, diced
freshly ground black pepper

TO SERVE
selection of crudités or blanched vegetables or halved hard-boiled eggs
thickly sliced good country bread

1. Drain the oil from the anchovies into a saucepan. Chop the anchovy fillets and add to the pan with the garlic and oil. Heat gently, mashing the anchovies until they dissolve, then cook until the garlic has softened and is beginning to colour.

2. Stir in the butter and add plenty of pepper. Pour into a small fondue pot or other small pot to put over the flame when serving.

3. Serve with long forks and stir the sauce when dipping the vegetables into it so that the anchovy and garlic mixture, which tends to settle at the bottom, is mixed in. Or you can spoon the sauce over the hard-boiled eggs.

CRISP MOZZARELLA FRITTERS

•

—— SERVES 2 ——

CORNMEAL gives a crisp, crunchy coating. To add extra flavour, try spreading a little pesto on the cheese slices or mixing some finely chopped herbs with the cornmeal. Frying the fritters quickly ensures that they come out crisp and 'dry' as the oil will not be absorbed. Serve as a snack, or with a crisp salad for a light main course.

1 egg, beaten
2 mozzarella cheeses, each weighing about 150g (5oz), cut into 1.25cm ($\frac{1}{2}$ inch) thick slices

50g (2oz) fine cornmeal
olive oil for deep frying
salt and freshly ground black pepper

1. Season the egg, then dip each slice of cheese in the egg. Coat the slices lightly and evenly with the cornmeal.

2. Two-thirds fill a deep-fat fryer or a deep frying pan with oil and heat to 180°C/350°F. Add the mozzarella slices and fry for 2–3 minutes until crisp and lightly browned.

3. Remove the slices and drain quickly on paper towels, if liked. Serve immediately.

MOZZARELLA IN CARROZZA

•

MADE from basic ingredients of bread, cheese, milk, flour and eggs this classic Neapolitan dish looks like an ordinary snack. But if it is as it should be – light and crisp on the outside, with delicious, just melting cheese that pulls into strings on the inside – it is far from ordinary. It is easy to achieve this perfection if you use a really good mozzarella (see page x), olive oil that is at the correct temperature for frying – and eat the sandwiches as soon as they are cooked. Serve as a snack, a first course or with a crisp salad for a light lunch.

olive oil for deep frying
8 thin slices of white bread, crusts removed, cut into 10 × 6.25cm (4 × 2½ inch) pieces
100ml (3½ fl oz) milk

1 fresh buffalo mozzarella, cut into 4 slices
6 tablespoons plain flour
2 eggs, beaten and seasoned
salt and freshly ground black pepper

1. Half-fill a deep-fat fryer or frying pan with oil and heat to 180°C/350°F.

2. Meanwhile, dip one side of a slice of bread briefly in milk, then place a cheese slice on the dry side. Grind pepper over.

3. Briefly dip one side of another slice of bread in milk, then place on the cheese, dry side down. Dust the 'sandwich' with flour then dip it in the egg. Allow the excess egg to drain off. Repeat with the remaining bread and cheese.

4. Fry the sandwiches in batches until golden and crisp on both sides. Using a slotted spoon, transfer to paper towels to drain. Serve the sandwiches immediately.

—— **VARIATIONS** ——

1. Top the cheese with chopped herbs, sliced black olives, sun-dried tomatoes or chopped anchovy fillets. Or spread the cheese with pesto, sun-dried tomato paste, black olive paste or anchovy paste.

VENETIAN SHRIMPS AND BEANS

•

—— SERVES 2–4 ——

I FIRST ate this dish in Venice, where it is made with the local speciality, *gamberetti*, fresh tiny, sweet shrimps. I have since had it a number of times all along the Adriatic coast; on one occasion it was made with crayfish. If fresh shrimps are not available, use fresh, juicy prawns (or crayfish); don't bother with frozen ones. The number the recipe serves depends on whether the dish is eaten as a first or main course.

a small piece each of carrot and
  celery
1 slice of lemon
about 550g (1¼lb) fresh shrimps or
  prawns in their shells
1 × 400g (14oz) can cannellini beans
2 well-flavoured tomatoes

1 clove garlic (optional)
3 tablespoons virgin olive oil
1 tablespoon lemon juice
2½ tablespoons chopped basil or a
  few torn rocket leaves
salt and freshly ground black pepper

1. Add the carrot, celery and lemon slice to a saucepan of water and bring to the boil. Add the shrimps or prawns, cover and quickly return to the boil. Boil for 2–4 minutes depending on the size of the shrimps or prawns.

2. Meanwhile, drain the beans, put into a saucepan, cover with water and heat through.

3. Chop the tomatoes. Chop the garlic, if used. Mix together the oil, lemon juice and seasoning.

4. Drain the shrimps or prawns, rinse under running cold water then peel. Cut large prawns into large pieces.

5. Drain the beans, then toss with the shrimps or prawns, the tomatoes, garlic and basil or rocket. Leave for 15–45 minutes before eating.

BRUSCHETTA WITH PARSLEY, SUN-DRIED TOMATO & OLIVE TOPPING

•

——— SERVES 4 ———

THE ORIGINAL Roman bruschetta is simply toasted bread (tradition-ally this would have been done over a charcoal fire) that is rubbed with a cut garlic clove and trickled with very good olive oil. Halved or chopped juicy tomatoes pressed into the bread before the oil is trickled over makes the simplest of authentic variations, *bruschetta al pomodoro*, but nowadays it is only one way of preparing bruschetta. This variation stays with the tomato theme but uses the sun-dried variety, combined with other store-cupboard ingredients plus parsley. It bursts with so much enervating flavour that no one would ever guess that it had been made quickly at a moment's notice.

1 tablespoon salt-packed capers, rinsed

6 halves of sun-dried tomatoes that have been packed in oil

50g (2oz) oil-cured black olives, stones removed

6 heaped tablespoons coarsely chopped parsley

1 red onion, thinly sliced

1 tablespoon oil from the sun-dried tomatoes

5 tablespoons extra virgin olive oil

4 slices of firm well-flavoured bread such as ciabatta or pugliese

freshly ground black pepper

1. Preheat the grill. Coarsely chop the capers, sun-dried tomatoes and olives and mix together, then toss with the parsley, onion, oil from the sun-dried tomatoes, olive oil and pepper.

2. Toast the bread on both sides. Pile the topping on to the bread and serve.

PARMESAN BRUSCHETTA

•

—— SERVES 4 ——

THIS recipe is really the Italian version of cheese on toast and is so simple that it hardly needs a recipe.

4 slices of firm well-flavoured bread
  such as ciabatta or pugliese
1 clove garlic
2–3 tablespoons extra virgin olive oil

about 65g (2½oz) freshly grated
  Parmesan cheese
freshly ground black pepper

1. Preheat the grill. Toast the bread until lightly browned on both sides.

2. Cut the garlic in half lengthways, then rub the cut side over one side of each slice of bread. Brush with olive oil and sprinkle with the cheese. Return to the grill for 1 minute until the cheese begins to melt. Grind the pepper over the cheese and serve straight away.

COURGETTE PIZZA ROLLS

•

—— SERVES 4 ——

I LOVE good pizzas and although an Italian would not class these rolls as pizzas they do rank alongside good ones. They also have the advantages of being cooked under the grill instead of in the oven and taking less time to cook.

4 tablespoons passata
100ml (3½fl oz) pesto
1 tablespoon virgin olive oil
1 clove garlic, crushed
4 ciabatta rolls or baps, halved

about 225g (½lb) small courgettes
olive oil for brushing
100g (3½oz) mozzarella cheese
a small handful of basil leaves
salt and freshly ground black pepper

1. Preheat the grill. Mix together the passata, pesto, virgin olive oil, garlic and seasoning and spread over the cut sides of the rolls or baps.

2. Thinly slice the courgettes diagonally and arrange in overlapping circles on the rolls or baps. Brush with olive oil, season with pepper and put under the grill for about 5 minutes until beginning to soften.

3. Thinly slice the cheese and put on the courgettes. Return to the grill until the cheese is bubbling.

4. Tear the basil leaves over the rolls or baps and grind more pepper over them.

ITALIAN BEANS ON GARLIC TOAST

•

—— SERVES 4 ——

ALTHOUGH I love these beans on toast for a quick and satisfying snack I also sometimes serve them (without the toast) as an accompaniment to grilled or fried meats or sausages, perhaps using just two slices of pancetta or bacon. You can substitute 2 tablespoons chopped rosemary for the thyme or parsley.

1 red onion, chopped
2 cloves garlic, crushed
4 slices of pancetta or bacon
2 tablespoons olive oil
1 tablespoon chopped thyme or
* parsley (optional)*

4 slices of firm bread
virgin olive oil for brushing
1 × 400g (14oz) can borlotti or
* cannellini beans*
salt and freshly ground black pepper

1. Preheat the grill. Finely chop the onion and crush the garlic. Chop the pancetta or bacon.

2. Heat the olive oil, add the onion, 1 crushed garlic clove and the pancetta or bacon and fry for 3–4 minutes, adding the thyme or parsley, if used, towards the end.

3. When the grill is hot, toast the bread on one side. Rub the other side with the remaining garlic, then brush with virgin olive oil and grill.

4. Drain, rinse and drain the beans. Add to the onion mixture with the seasoning and heat through. Spoon on to the toast and serve.

POACHED EGG WITH FONTINA CHEESE ON TOAST

•

──── SERVES 2–4 ────

Fontina cheese is made from the milk of cows that have grazed on the lush herb-and flower-strewn summer pastures of the Alps so it is not surprising that the cheese has a deliciously sweet flavour that, though mild, is distinctive. It has a semi-soft texture that melts unctuously when heated. The bread and eggs are fried in the original Piedmontese dish, but I prefer the less greasy result obtained by toasting and poaching them respectively.

4 anchovy fillets	25g (1oz) butter, diced
4 slices of firm bread	freshly ground black pepper
4 eggs	chopped parsley to serve
4 slices fontina cheese	

1. Preheat the grill. Chop the anchovy fillets.

2. Toast one side of each slice of bread. Turn the grill to moderately low.

3. Meanwhile, bring a frying pan of water to simmering point, carefully break the eggs into it, then poach for about 3 minutes or until set to your liking. Spoon hot water over the yolks during cooking.

4. Lay a slice of cheese on the untoasted sides of the bread and put under the grill until melted. Turn off the grill and top each slice of cheese with half a chopped anchovy fillet; leave under the grill.

5. Melt the butter in a small pan, then add the remaining anchovies, mashing until dissolved. Season with pepper.

6. Put an egg on each slice of bread and pour the anchovy sauce over. Sprinkle with chopped parsley.

BROAD BEAN AND GOAT'S CHEESE FRITTATA

•

—— SERVES 2 with a side salad and crusty bread ——

I PREFER to leave a frittata slightly moist, but you can set its top by putting the pan under a preheated grill.

175g (6oz) shelled fresh young broad
  beans or thawed frozen beans
4 eggs
2 teaspoons finely chopped dill

a knob of unsalted butter
about 65g (2½oz) goat's cheese
salt and freshly ground black pepper

1. Cook the broad beans in boiling salted water until tender. Drain well.

2. Using a fork, lightly beat the eggs with the dill and seasoning until the yolks and whites are blended. Stir in the broad beans.

3. Heat the butter in a heavy frying pan about 20–22.5cm (8–9 inches) in diameter until beginning to foam. Pour in the egg mixture, turn the heat down to very low and cook for about 15 minutes until the bulk of the eggs is set but the top is still creamy. Scatter the cheese over and serve.

4. If liked, put the pan under a preheated grill to set the top of the frittata.

A frittata is usually described as an Italian omelette, but this can be misleading as it is quite unlike the classic French dish (except that it is made from eggs). Frittate are thick, the filling is contained within the egg mixture, they are cooked slowly, are easy to make for a number of people and are often cut into wedges for serving. They are natural vehicles for all manner of fillings, planned or impromptu as the occasion demands: chopped sausages, cured meats, chicken, fish and shellfish, vegetables, cheese, herbs or store-cupboard ingredients such as sun-dried tomatoes, capers or anchovy fillets.

COURGETTE FRITTATA

•

——— SERVES 2 ———

It is important to use small courgettes; not only will they have the best flavour but they will be firm and will not exude a lot of moisture when cooked. If you only have large courgettes you can prevent them becoming watery when cooked by slicing, grating or chopping them as appropriate, then sprinkling them with salt and leaving for about 20 minutes. Rinse well and pat dry before using.

1 tablespoon olive oil
225g ($\frac{1}{2}$lb) small courgettes, coarsely grated
4 eggs
3 tablespoons freshly grated Parmesan cheese

1 tablespoon chopped parsley
1 tablespoon chopped basil
15g ($\frac{1}{2}$oz) unsalted butter
salt and freshly ground black pepper

1. Heat the oil in a heavy frying pan 20–22.5cm (8–9 inches) in diameter, add the courgettes and fry until light brown.

2. Meanwhile, using a fork, lightly beat together the Parmesan, herbs and seasoning until the yolks and whites are blended.

3. If the courgettes have produced a lot of moisture, raise the heat and boil it off. Add the butter to the pan. When it is foaming turn down the heat to very low and stir in the egg mixture. Cook for about 15 minutes until the bulk of the eggs is set but the top is still creamy.

4. If liked, put the pan under a preheated grill to set the top of the frittata.

Basil Frittata

•

—— SERVES 4 ——

THIS is about as simple a frittata as you can get, but it is one of my favourites; when fresh basil is at its most fragrant I think it *is* my favourite frittata.

6 eggs
3 tablespoons freshly grated
  Parmesan cheese

4 tablespoons torn basil leaves
40g (1½oz) unsalted butter
salt and freshly ground black pepper

1. Using a fork, lightly beat the eggs with the cheese, basil and seasoning until the yolks and whites are blended.

2. Heat the butter in a heavy frying pan 25cm (10 inches) in diameter, over a moderate heat, until beginning to foam. Pour in the egg mixture, turn the heat down to very low and cook for about 15 minutes until the bulk of the eggs is set but the top is still creamy.

3. If liked, put the pan under a preheated grill to set the top of the frittata.

ASPARAGUS WITH EGGS AND PARMESAN CHEESE

•

——— SERVES 2 ———

THIS IS really an adult version of Marmite soldiers, the asparagus spears being dipped in butter, then egg yolk and Parmesan cheese (which should not be too strongly flavoured or it will dominate the asparagus and egg). The eggs can be fried, poached or hard-boiled but the yolks *must* be soft – you can't dip an asparagus tip into a hard yolk! To make the dish more filling, use four eggs and increase the asparagus to 450g (1lb). Italians would use fat, white asparagus but I think slim, green English spears really are much better for this recipe – and they cook more quickly.

300g (10oz) slim asparagus spears   *a knob of unsalted butter, diced*
2 eggs   *freshly grated Parmesan cheese*

1. Bring a tall saucepan of salted water to the boil. If the asparagus stems are thick the skin of the lower parts of the stems may be tough; if so, use a potato peeler to shave it off. Group the asparagus into 2 bundles and tie at the bottom and beneath the tips. Add to the pan and cover with a lid or a dome of foil. Boil for 10–15 minutes.

2. Meanwhile, cook the eggs by your preferred method, and gently melt the butter in a small non-stick saucepan.

3. Remove the asparagus from the water, untie the bundles and briefly spread the spears out between 2 thick layers of paper towels.

4. Put the asparagus on 2 warm plates and add the eggs. Either pour the butter over the asparagus tips or serve it in a warmed small bowl for dipping. Serve the Parmesan in another small bowl. Also add a pepper grinder, and napkins.

BASIL AND HARD-BOILED EGGS IN PARMA HAM PARCELS

•

—— SERVES 4 ——

THIS lovely dish is a very successful Italian version of the ever-popular combination of ham and eggs. Convention says that the eggs should be placed cut-side down but I think the parcels are nicer to eat if the yolks are uppermost – it's very easy to prop up the parcels so that they don't fall over.

4 large eggs, at room temperature
12 small basil leaves
8 thin slices of Parma ham

extra virgin olive oil for trickling
freshly ground black pepper

1. Fill a saucepan that is just large enough to hold the eggs with water. Bring to the boil, then lower in the eggs on a spoon and simmer for 6–7 minutes for firm whites and soft yolks, 10–12 minutes for firm whites and yolks.

2. Drain the eggs and rinse under running cold water. Peel them and cut them in half lengthways. Tear one basil leaf over each half-egg, then season with pepper. Wrap in a slice of Parma ham. Trickle virgin olive oil over the top. Tear the remaining basil leaves and sprinkle them over the egg parcels.

EGGS WITH TUNA SAUCE

•

—— SERVES 2–4 ——

Tuna sauce is so quick and delicious it is a shame to restrict its use to its traditional place in *Vitello tonnato* (cold poached veal with tuna sauce). In fact, the sauce goes equally well, if not better, with boiled eggs, making a dish that is practical and economical for cooks who have time to spare as well as being useful for those in a hurry. You will probably find that the quantity of sauce is too much for four eggs (it could be served with six); the remainder can be kept in a covered container in the refrigerator for two days and used with more hard-boiled eggs, as a dip for crudités or as a pasta sauce. The more usual way of serving the eggs is, as here, on a bed of lettuce leaves, which is appropriate for a first course. I also like to arrange them on good wholemeal or rye bread before spooning the sauce over them, perhaps adding a tomato salad as an accompaniment. I cook the eggs so that the yolks are still soft and creamy when I eat them this way.

4 large eggs, at room temperature
1 × 200g (7oz) can tuna packed in
   olive oil
4 anchovy fillets
115ml (4fl oz) mayonnaise
2 tablespoons capers

1½–2 tablespoons lemon juice
freshly ground black pepper
crisp lettuce leaves
chopped parsley and good bread to
   serve

1. Fill a saucepan that is just large enough to hold the eggs with water. Bring to the boil, then lower in the eggs on a spoon. Simmer for 6–7 minutes for firm whites and soft yolks, 10–12 minutes for firm whites and yolks.

2. Meanwhile, put the tuna with its oil, the anchovy fillets, mayonnaise and capers in a blender or food processor. Mix until smooth, then add lemon juice and pepper to taste. Make a small bed of lettuce leaves on each of 2 or 4 plates.

3. Drain the eggs and rinse under running cold water. Peel them and cut them in half lengthways. Put 2 or 3 halves, cut-side down, on each plate. Spoon the sauce over and sprinkle with parsley. Serve with good bread.

CHAPTER TWO

Vegetables & Salads

Vegetables play an important part in the Italian diet. Not only do they accompany the meat, fish or poultry, but a vegetable dish may actually be the main course, a custom that is becoming more prevalent in Britain. No matter how simple the recipe – Courgettes with Oregano (see page 41) is an example – it always tastes good. This is because Italians buy vegetables that are in peak condition, full of flavour and very fresh, and know how to use them to their best advantage. The secrets of good cooking can be passed on but unless produce of a similar quality is used, it is impossible to create dishes that taste as wonderful as they do in Italy.

With the greatly expanded range of salad leaves and flavouring ingredients that is now available, it is possible to make exciting and varied Italian-style salads. Some are suitable accompaniments to main courses, but others make good first courses in themselves, while yet others are ideal for a light meal, perhaps preceded by a soup and served with good bread.

GRILLED ARTICHOKE SALAD

•

—— SERVES 4 ——

LARGE artichoke hearts preserved in oil can be bought loose from Italian food shops and good delicatessens. Alternatively, you can use artichokes from a jar of artichoke hearts in oil. If you do, some of the oil can be used for this salad and the remainder kept for other salads or tossing with pasta. Do *not* use artichokes in brine.

8 large artichokes preserved in oil
4 Little Gem lettuces or lettuce
  hearts
5 tablespoons olive oil or a mixture
  of oil from the artichokes and olive
  oil

1 tablespoon lemon juice
salt and freshly ground black pepper

1. Preheat the grill. Cut the artichokes in half from top to bottom. Lay the artichoke halves on the grill rack and brown under the grill.

2. Meanwhile, divide the lettuces into leaves and arrange on a serving plate. Whisk together the oil, lemon juice and seasoning and spoon over the lettuce leaves.

3. Add the artichoke hearts to the plate.

WINTER PANZANELLA

•

SERVES 2

PANZANELLA is a classic bread salad from Tuscany. Its success lies with the quality of the bread and really flavourful tomatoes. If I cannot get the latter I use sun-dried tomatoes and the oil in which they have been kept to make a quick, simplified variation. It is still important, though, to use good Italian bread, which is now available from many bakers and supermarkets.

4 slices of ciabatta
about 8 oil-cured black olives
12 sun-dried tomatoes in oil
a handful of rocket or young spinach
  leaves

about 5 tablespoons oil from the sun-
  dried tomatoes
1 tablespoon red wine vinegar
salt and freshly ground black pepper

1. Soak the bread in cold water for 5–10 minutes.

2. Meanwhile, halve the olives, removing the stones, if liked, and chop the sun-dried tomatoes. Tear the rocket or spinach leaves into a salad bowl.

3. Drain the bread and squeeze out as much water as possible. Add to the bowl, scatter the olives and sun-dried tomatoes over and mix everything together.

4. Using a fork, whisk together the oil from the sun-dried tomatoes, vinegar and seasoning, pour over the salad and toss to mix well; if the salad is too dry, add some more oil.

MUSHROOM AND PARMESAN CHEESE SALAD

•

——— SERVES 4 ———

Some people like to serve this salad as soon as it has been made but others prefer to leave it for a while; for me, it is a question of how I feel, and the amount of time available.

300g (10oz) porcini (cep), oyster or
   large brown cap mushrooms,
   thinly sliced
65g (2½oz) piece of Parmesan cheese
10 basil leaves, torn

3 tablespoons virgin olive oil
1 tablespoon lemon juice
salt and freshly ground black pepper

1. Arrange the mushrooms on a large serving plate. Using a potato peeler, shave strips of Parmesan cheese over the mushrooms. Scatter the basil over.

2. Using a fork, whisk together the oil, lemon juice and seasoning. Pour over the salad. Serve at once or leave for up to 30 minutes.

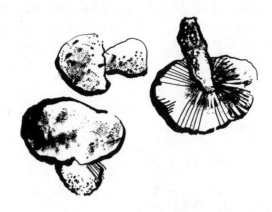

Warm Mushroom and Pancetta Salad

•

No pancetta? Use thick-cut smoked streaky bacon. No balsamic vinegar? Substitute $\frac{3}{4}$ tablespoon tarragon vinegar for both vinegars. Serve as a first course or as an accompaniment to Chicken with Rosemary and Lemon (see page 89) or Pork with Sage (see page 98).

75g (3oz) pancetta, cut into strips
1 clove garlic
350g (12oz) oyster or brown cap
  mushrooms
3 tablespoons virgin olive oil
2 good handfuls of salad leaves
  including rocket and spinach

chopped tarragon, chervil, basil or
  parsley (optional)
$\frac{1}{2}$ tablespoon balsamic vinegar
$\frac{1}{2}$ tablespoon white wine vinegar
salt and freshly ground black pepper

1. Heat a heavy frying pan, add the pancetta and fry until the fat runs. Increase the heat and cook until crisp.

2. Meanwhile, crush the garlic with a pinch of salt, then chop it. Break the mushrooms into pieces.

3. Using a slotted spoon, transfer the pancetta to paper towels. Add the oil, garlic, mushrooms and seasoning to the pan and cook for 3–4 minutes until just tender.

4. Divide the salad leaves between 4 plates.

5. Quickly tip the pancetta, and herbs if using, on to the mushrooms then, using a slotted spoon, lift from the pan and scatter over the salad leaves.

6. Quickly stir the vinegars into the pan and boil for 1–2 minutes. Pour over the salads and serve immediately.

FENNEL AND RICOTTA SALAD

•

—— SERVES 4 ——

THE CRISP aniseed flavour of small fennel bulbs marries well with the delicate but definite taste of ricotta cheese. Their flavour is subtler and less coarse than that of large bulbs and their texture is also finer. This is particularly important when they are eaten. The bulbs must, of course, be fresh and shiny. Serve as a first course.

450g (1lb) small fennel bulbs
½ clove garlic
1½–2 tablespoons lemon juice

6 tablespoons virgin olive oil
115g (4oz) ricotta cheese
salt and freshly ground black pepper

1. Very thinly slice the fennel; reserve the feathery green fronds. Put the fennel in a shallow serving dish.

2. Crush the garlic with a pinch of salt, then whisk with the lemon juice, oil and pepper. Pour over the fennel.

3. Break up the ricotta cheese with a fork and spoon on to the fennel. Toss lightly. Snip the reserved fronds over the salad.

—— **VARIATION** ——

For Fennel and Gorgonzola Salad, substitute Gorgonzola for the ricotta cheese and sprinkle some chopped walnuts, if liked, over the salad.

COURGETTE AND PARMESAN SALAD

•

—— SERVES 2–4 ——

THIS beautifully light, fresh-tasting salad is one of my summertime favourites. It can be served as a light first course in an all-over light meal or before a more substantial or rich main course. A few mint or parsley leaves can be added for an additional flavour.

225g ($\frac{1}{2}$lb) small courgettes
50g (2oz) piece of Parmesan cheese
3 tablespoons lemon juice

5 tablespoons extra virgin or virgin
  olive oil
salt and freshly ground black pepper

1. Using a mandoline or food processor, slice the courgettes very thinly. Arrange the slices on a serving plate so that they overlap slightly.

2. Using a potato peeler, shave the Parmesan into thin slivers and scatter them over the courgettes.

3. Whisk together the lemon juice, oil and seasoning, then pour the dressing over the cheese and courgettes. Serve straight away.

WARM ROCKET, CHEESE AND POTATO SALAD

•

FOR THE cheese you can use taleggio, which is a mild, creamy, young cheese from northern Italy, a buttery Gorgonzola (but not a strong, piquant one) or a creamy Dolcelatte. If you do not have any rocket, young spinach leaves can be used instead, but they are not quite as good. Serve the salad as a snack or first course, or in larger portions for a light meal.

350g (12oz) small new potatoes
about 175g (6oz) mild Italian blue
   cheese
a large handful of rocket leaves

1 tablespoon hazelnut or walnut oil
1 tablespoon extra virgin olive oil
salt and freshly ground black pepper

1. Cook the potatoes in boiling salted water until tender.

2. Meanwhile, coarsely chop the cheese. Tear the rocket into large pieces and divide between 2–3 individual salad bowls.

3. Drain the potatoes, quickly cut them into approximate halves and add to the salad bowls. Scatter the cheese over the bowls, pour the oils over and toss everything together. Grind pepper over the salads and serve.

ROCKET, TOMATO AND MOZZARELLA SALAD

•

—— SERVES 2 ——

THE DISTINCTIVE flavour of rocket marries well with the sweet juiciness of the tomatoes and the mild creaminess of mozzarella to make a sophisticated but simple-tasting salad. Little Gem lettuce or radicchio can be used instead of rocket.

a good handful of rocket leaves
150g (5oz) buffalo mozzarella
    cheese, chopped
8 cherry tomatoes, halved

3 tablespoons virgin olive oil
scant 1 tablespoon white wine
    vinegar
salt and freshly ground black pepper

1. Divide the rocket between 2 plates. Scatter the cheese and tomatoes over it. Coarsely grind the pepper over the salads.

2. Using a fork, whisk together the oil, vinegar and salt. Pour the dressing over the salads and toss to mix.

TOMATO, MOZZARELLA AND BASIL SALAD

•

—— SERVES 2 ——

ALTHOUGH in concept this is the hackneyed and abused *salade Caprese* of Italian restaurants, in execution, when you have really well-flavoured tomatoes and genuine buffalo mozzarella, it is a rare treat, and so quick and simple; if you do not have these ingredients, forget it.

1–2 balls of buffalo mozzarella
  cheese, thinly sliced
450g (1lb) well-flavoured, very ripe
  tomatoes, thinly sliced

about 15 basil leaves
2–3 tablespoons extra virgin olive oil
salt and freshly ground black pepper

1. Arrange the cheese and tomatoes on 2 plates so that they overlap.

2. Scatter the basil leaves over them, sprinkle with the seasoning and trickle the oil over the salad.

BEAN AND TUNA SALAD

•

*F*AGIOLI E TONNATO (bean and tuna salad) is one of the classic antipasti dishes, and additions to the basic beans and tuna are many and various – you can add black olives, chopped anchovy fillets, capers or chopped red pepper. I sometimes use pesto diluted with a little extra virgin olive oil and lemon juice as a dressing.

1 clove garlic
6 tablespoons extra virgin olive oil
2–3 tablespoons lemon juice
1–1½ × 400g (14oz) can cannellini or
  white kidney beans, drained and
  rinsed

1 red onion, finely chopped
1 × 200g (7oz) can tuna in oil, drained
  and coarsely flaked
salt and freshly ground black pepper
chopped parsley for garnish

1. Crush the garlic with a pinch of salt, then whisk with the oil, lemon juice and pepper, using a fork.

2. Mix together the beans, onion and tuna, then pour the dressing over them and toss together. Sprinkle with chopped parsley.

PRAWN SALAD WITH COURGETTES AND MINT

•

—— SERVES 2 ——

THE COOL pink, red, cream and green colours correctly signal this to be an inviting light salad. It is one of the few Italian recipes that makes use of mint.

juice of 1 lemon	$\frac{1}{2}$ *red pepper*
4 tablespoons virgin olive oil	*225g ($\frac{1}{2}$lb) peeled cooked prawns*
1 tablespoon chopped parsley	*about 8 mint leaves*
175g (6oz) small courgettes	*salt and freshly ground black pepper*

1. Mix together the lemon juice, oil, parsley and seasoning.

2. Cut the courgettes into thin matchsticks. Cut the pepper into thin slices and cut across the slices to halve them.

3. Toss the vegetables with the prawns, mint leaves and dressing. Chill, if possible, for 10–30 minutes.

COURGETTES WITH OREGANO

•

—— SERVES 4 ——

I LIKE to serve good crusty bread with this to mop up the cooking juices.

5 tablespoons virgin olive oil

2 cloves garlic

575g (1¼lb) small courgettes

about ½ teaspoon dried oregano

1 lemon, halved

salt and freshly ground black pepper

1. Heat the oil in large frying pan. Coarsely chop the garlic, add to the pan and fry until lightly browned.

2. Meanwhile, thinly slice the courgettes.

3. Stir the courgettes into the pan, add the oregano and pepper and fry over a medium–high heat, stirring frequently, for about 10 minutes until the courgettes are tender but still firm to the bite.

4. Add salt and lemon juice to taste, and serve the courgettes with the cooking juices.

GLAZED LEEKS WITH PARMESAN CHEESE

•

—— SERVES 4 ——

ITALIANS overcome the problem of watery leeks by cooking them in butter and just enough water to cover, then boiling away the water at the end of cooking so that they are lightly glazed. A final addition of Parmesan cheese completes a beautiful dish.

40g (1½oz) unsalted butter, diced
6 medium leeks, split lengthways

3 tablespoons freshly grated
  Parmesan cheese
salt and freshly ground black pepper

1. Heat the butter in a frying pan or shallow flameproof casserole large enough to hold the leeks in a single layer.

2. Add the leeks and enough water to just cover them. Bring to the boil, then cover the pan and cook over a medium–low heat for about 15 minutes, turning the leeks occasionally, until they are tender when pierced with a fork.

3. Uncover the pan and boil away the liquid; the leeks should become slightly glazed and golden. Lightly stir in the Parmesan cheese and seasoning, then serve.

BROCCOLI WITH CHILLI AND GARLIC

•

—— SERVES 4 ——

VARIATIONS to this recipe are: frying some pine nuts until pale golden before adding the garlic and chilli; cutting the garlic into fine slivers and frying it until it becomes light golden before adding the chilli; adding chopped anchovy fillets or sun-dried tomatoes; scattering shaved or finely grated Parmesan cheese over the broccoli just before serving.

675g (1½lb) broccoli
3 tablespoons virgin olive oil
2–3 cloves garlic, finely chopped

1 dried red chilli, seeded and
 chopped
salt

1. Bring a large saucepan of salted water to the boil. Separate the broccoli florets from the stalks. Cut the stalks into 1.25cm (½ inch) thick diagonal slices and add to the boiling water. Cover and quickly return to the boil. After 2 minutes boiling add the florets, cover and simmer for 2–3 minutes.

2. Meanwhile, heat the oil in a large frying pan, add the garlic and chilli and fry until fragrant.

3. Drain the broccoli well (toss carefully in the colander to shake off water droplets). Add to the frying pan and stir everything together.

FENNEL WITH PARMESAN CHEESE

•

—— SERVES 4 ——

IN FLORENCE, fennel used to be eaten at the end of a meal as it was believed to help digestion and was therefore an antidote to heavy or rich food. The practice has virtually died out, except in a few places in Tuscany where sliced fennel is sometimes served as a *digestif*, perhaps accompanied by fresh oranges or mandarins. This is a more usual way of eating fennel.

4 young fennel bulbs
40g (1½oz) unsalted butter, diced
½ lemon

50g (2oz) freshly grated Parmesan
  cheese
salt and freshly ground black pepper

1. Bring a saucepan of water to the boil. Meanwhile, cut the fennel bulbs into quarters vertically. Reserve the feathery green fronds for garnish. Add the fennel quarters to the water and boil until tender but still slightly crisp. Drain well.

2. While the fennel is cooking, preheat the grill. Put the butter into a shallow baking dish large enough to hold the fennel in a tightly-packed single layer, and put under the grill to melt.

3. Drain the fennel well, then tip into the dish. Turn to coat with butter, squeeze the lemon over, then season and sprinkle with the cheese. Put under the grill until golden and bubbling.

HERB-TOPPED TOMATOES

•

—— SERVES 2 – 4 ——

IF YOU have the oven on for another dish, such as Italian Stuffed Mushrooms (see page 13), you could put the tomatoes into it either when you remove the mushrooms, or a little before, then lower the oven temperature to 180°C/350°F/Gas Mark 4 and bake them for about 15 minutes. The insides of the tomatoes can be used in sauces, soups or casseroles.

2 large tomatoes
3 tablespoons fresh breadcrumbs
2 tablespoons coarsely grated
* Parmesan cheese*
1 clove garlic, finely chopped

1½ tablespoons chopped parsley
1 tablespoon chopped basil
olive oil for trickling
salt and freshly ground black pepper

1. Preheat the grill.

2. Cut the tomatoes in half horizontally. Scoop out the insides and sprinkle the insides of the tomato shells with salt. Leave upside down on paper towels to drain while the grill heats up.

3. Mix together the breadcrumbs, Parmesan, garlic, herbs and seasoning.

4. Put the tomatoes, cut-side up, in a shallow baking dish. Pile the herb mixture into the tomatoes, trickle over a little olive oil, then put under the grill for about 15 minutes until the tomatoes are tender to your liking.

Italian Sautéed Mushrooms

•

THIS IS a basic recipe for sautéed mushrooms, *trifolati* in Italy. It can be embellished by adding, for example, anchovy fillets for a deep, savoury flavour, or wine, chopped tomatoes and/or chopped onion. Or grated Parmesan cheese can be sprinkled over the mushrooms to serve. Basil, thyme or rosemary can be substituted for the parsley.

4 tablespoons virgin olive oil
$1\frac{1}{2}$–2 cloves garlic, finely chopped
675g ($1\frac{1}{2}$lb) brown cap mushrooms

3 tablespoons finely chopped
  parsley
salt and freshly ground black pepper

1. Heat the oil in a frying pan large enough to hold the mushrooms without crowding them. Add the garlic and cook until lightly coloured but not brown.

2. Meanwhile, slice the mushrooms. Add to the coloured garlic and fry, shaking the pan and stirring the mushrooms frequently, for about 5 minutes; do not overcook.

3. Stir in the parsley and seasoning.

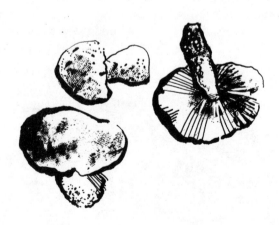

FLORENTINE MUSHROOMS WITH SAVOURY TOMATO SAUCE

•

—— SERVES 4 ——

T HE MUSHROOMS should have a subtle deep, savoury, almost meaty flavour. This can be achieved by cooking them slowly for a long time, but this Florentine recipe produces the same result very quickly by following the simple old custom of adding anchovies to dishes to enhance their flavour.

3 tablespoons virgin olive oil
½ red onion or 1 shallot, finely
   chopped
1 plump clove garlic
450g (1lb) brown cap mushrooms

2 well-flavoured tomatoes
5 anchovy fillets
1½ tablespoons chopped parsley
freshly ground black pepper

1. Heat the oil in a large frying pan, add the onion or shallot and cook until softened.

2. Meanwhile, finely chop the garlic and halve or quarter the mushrooms. Add the garlic to the pan, cook for about 1 minute until fragrant, then add the mushrooms and cook, stirring occasionally, until the juices have evaporated.

3. While the mushrooms are cooking, seed and chop the tomatoes (peel them first if you like). Coarsely chop the anchovies.

4. Push the mushrooms away from one part of the pan. Add the anchovies to the bare area and mash them with a wooden spoon. Add the tomatoes and most of the parsley and stir everything together. Simmer gently for about 5 minutes.

5. Season generously with black pepper; salt will probably not be necessary because of the saltiness of the anchovies. Serve sprinkled with the remaining parsley.

FRESH SPINACH WITH PARMESAN CHEESE

•

—— SERVES 4 ——

LIGHT, quickly cooked Spinach with Parmesan Cheese is one of the most quintessentially Italian of all dishes. It can really only be made with fresh spinach leaves, which preferably should be small and young. Fortunately, with all the changes there have been in vegetable growing and packing in recent years, this is now a possibility for many of us for much of the year.

900g (2lb) small spinach leaves
50g (2oz) unsalted butter
freshly grated nutmeg

about 40g (1½oz) freshly grated
   Parmesan cheese
salt and freshly ground black pepper

1. Wash but do not dry the spinach, simply shake off excess moisture.

2. Melt the butter in a saucepan, add the spinach with just the water clinging to the leaves and cook, stirring occasionally, for 2–3 minutes until the spinach is tender.

3. Season with a little salt, plenty of pepper and a pinch of nutmeg. Sprinkle with the Parmesan and serve.

SICILIAN SPINACH WITH PINE NUTS AND RAISINS

•

—— SERVES 4 ——

THE USE of pine nuts and raisins, or sultanas or currants, pinpoints this as being a typically Sicilian dish.

900g (2lb) small spinach leaves
3 tablespoons virgin olive oil
1 clove garlic, crushed
4 tablespoons pine nuts

3 tablespoons raisins
juice of $\frac{1}{2}$ lemon (optional)
salt and freshly ground black pepper

1. Wash but do not dry the spinach, simply shake off excess moisture. Put the spinach into a large saucepan with just the last of the water clinging to the leaves and cook, stirring occasionally, until wilted. Drain well.

2. Meanwhile, heat the oil in a frying pan, add the garlic and fry until golden. Remove and add the pine nuts.

3. When the nuts are brown, stir in the raisins, then add the spinach, seasoning, and lemon juice if used. Stir together and serve.

CAULIFLOWER WITH OLIVES AND ANCHOVIES

•

—— SERVES 4 ——

A SIMPLE treatment that turns cauliflower into a piquant, savoury vegetable accompaniment for grilled lamb or pork.

1 small onion
450g (1lb) cauliflower florets
¾ × 50g (2oz) can anchovy fillets
1 plump clove garlic

25g (1oz) pitted black olives
1 tablespoon capers
1½ tablespoons chopped parsley
freshly ground black pepper

1. Bring a large saucepan of water to the boil. Finely chop the onion.

2. Add the cauliflower to the saucepan, cover and return quickly to the boil. Boil for 5–7 minutes until just tender.

3. Meanwhile, drain the oil from the anchovies into a smallish frying pan, heat, then add the onion and fry until softened.

4. Crush the garlic to a paste with the anchovies. Stir into the frying pan with the olives, capers, parsley and pepper. Heat through gently.

5. Drain the cauliflower and turn into a warm serving dish. Pour the anchovy mixture over the cauliflower and toss lightly.

Braised Radicchio with Pancetta

•

—— SERVES 4 ——

Cooking radicchio gives it a richer flavour. However, this gain is at the expense of its beautiful, characteristic burgundy colour and distinctive white markings as it becomes tawny red. Serve the radicchio with good bread to mop up juices.

2 tablespoons virgin olive oil
50g (2oz) pancetta or thick-cut
  streaky bacon, diced
½ small onion, finely chopped
1 clove garlic, finely chopped

2 heads of radicchio
2 tablespoons red wine vinegar
1 tablespoon balsamic vinegar
1 teaspoon caster sugar
salt and freshly ground black pepper

1. Heat the oil in a large frying pan. Add the pancetta or bacon and cook for a minute or two. Add the onion and garlic and continue to cook until the bacon is browned at the edges and the onion is soft.

2. Meanwhile, divide each radicchio head into 8 wedges, cut through the core.

3. Stir the vinegars, sugar and 3 tablespoons water into the pan, then add the raddichio, packing it in a single layer. Bring to the boil, then cover and cook for about 12 minutes, turning the raddichio over halfway through. If there is too much liquid at the end of cooking, remove the lid and cook gently until the liquid is reduced. Season and serve warm.

SAUTÉED RED PEPPERS

•

—— SERVES 4 ——

SAUTÉEING red peppers brings out their sweetness, which is further enhanced by a judicious splash of sweet-sharp balsamic vinegar. This makes a good accompaniment to Lamb Cutlets Grilled with Herbs (see page 104) or Red Mullet with Parma Ham and Basil or Sage (see page 81).

3 tablespoons olive oil
1 large red onion, thinly sliced
1 clove garlic
2 fleshy red peppers

$1\frac{1}{2}$ teaspoons balsamic vinegar
chopped basil or parsley for serving
salt and freshly ground black pepper

1. Heat the oil in a large frying pan, add the onion and fry until softened but not coloured.

2. Meanwhile, chop the garlic and thinly slice the peppers.

3. Add the peppers to the pan and fry briskly until tender and browned in patches. Add the garlic about halfway through the cooking.

4. Pour the contents of the pan into a warm serving dish and sprinkle with the balsamic vinegar, basil or parsley and seasoning.

BRAISED CELERY WITH PANCETTA AND TOMATOES

•

—— SERVES 4 ——

FOR EVEN cooking choose celery sticks that are all the same size – I prefer to use medium-sized ones. However, if you are using heads of celery and therefore have celery sticks of different sizes, start cooking the fatter sticks before adding the slimmer ones.

4 tablespoons olive oil
2 onions, thinly slices
50g (2oz) pancetta or unsmoked bacon
2 well-flavoured tomatoes
450g (1lb) celery sticks

1–2 halves of sun-dried tomato, sliced (optional)
salt and freshly ground black pepper
black olives, preferably oil-cured, or chopped parsley for garnish

1. Heat the oil in a flameproof shallow casserole or deep frying pan, add the onions and cook until softened and lightly coloured.

2. Meanwhile, cut the pancetta or bacon into strips, chop the tomatoes and cut the celery sticks into 7.5cm (3 inch) lengths.

3. Add the pancetta or bacon to the pan and cook briskly until the fat becomes translucent.

4. Stir in the tomatoes and their seeds and juice, the sun-dried tomatoes, if using, and the celery sticks and seasoning. Cover and cook over a moderate heat for about 20 minutes, shaking the pan occasionally, until the celery is tender. If the liquid is too runny and abundant towards the end of cooking, remove the lid, increase the heat and stir while boiling the water away.

5. Serve garnished with black olives or chopped parsley.

CHAPTER THREE

Pastas & Pizzas

THE conventional place for pasta is as a first course, but today's less structured meals and more casual life styles, coupled with an ever-widening range of pasta recipes, mean that pasta dishes now are also served as snacks, main courses or with meat, poultry and fish.

Pizzas make marvellous snacks or main courses. Pre-packaged ready-made bases may not be as good as home-made ones, but if you add plenty of good, tasty topping ingredients they provide the starting-point for what can be quickly prepared and interesting snacks or main courses for the expenditure of very little effort or time.

To help ensure that cooked pasta has a good texture and prevent it sticking, allow 575ml (1 pint) water to each 115g (4oz) pasta. Bring the water to a rolling boil. If you boil it in an electric kettle, don't forget that the water will cool when it is poured into the saucepan – you can reduce the re-boiling time by putting the pan over a low heat before adding the water so that it begins to warm up. Add the pasta in one go, give it a stir with a fork to separate it, then cover the pan and bring the water to the boil again as quickly as possible. After that, uncover the pan and cook the pasta until it is just tender but still firm to the bite. The time that this takes will depend on whether the pasta is fresh or dried, its thickness and shape, and the brand.

SPAGHETTI WITH GARLIC CRUMBS

•

—— SERVES 2–4 ——

A SIMPLE but surprisingly effective pasta dish. The number of people it serves depends on whether it is to be eaten as a snack or light meal, or as a first course or accompaniment to another dish like Steak Pizzaiola (see page 107).

2–3 tablespoons virgin olive oil
2 cloves garlic, crushed
about 75g (3oz) fresh breadcrumbs
350g (12oz) spaghetti
a handful of chopped herbs such as
  parsley, tarragon, basil or chervil

salt and coarsely ground black
  pepper
freshly grated Parmesan cheese to
  serve

1. Heat 2 tablespoons of the oil in a frying pan, add the garlic and breadcrumbs and fry, stirring frequently, until the crumbs are crisp and brown; add a little more oil if necessary and take care that the garlic and breadcrumbs do not burn.

2. Meanwhile, bring a large saucepan of salted water to the boil. Add the spaghetti, stir, then cover the pan and return quickly to the boil. Remove the lid and cook for 3–4 minutes if fresh, about 8 minutes if dried, until tender but still firm to the bite.

3. Drain the spaghetti and toss with the herbs and pepper. Scatter the breadcrumbs over the spaghetti, toss briefly and serve with freshly grated Parmesan.

HERB AND PECORINO OR PARMESAN CARBONARA

•

THE residual heat in the pasta and pan should be sufficient to cook the egg so that it gives a thick, creamy coating to the tagliatelle, but if you like you can put the pan over a very low heat; be careful, though, that the egg does not overcook.

300–350g (10–12oz) tagliatelle
6 tablespoons extra virgin olive oil
75g (3oz) freshly grated pecorino or
   Parmesan cheese
4 egg yolks

2 cloves garlic, crushed
2 tablespoons chopped chives
2 tablespoons chopped basil
2 tablespoons chopped marjoram
freshly ground black pepper

1. Bring a large saucepan of salted water to the boil. Add the tagliatelle, stir, then cover the pan and quickly return to the boil. Remove the lid and cook for 3–5 minutes if fresh, 5–6 minutes if dried, until tender but still firm to the bite.

2. Meanwhile, mix together the oil, cheese, egg yolks, garlic, herbs and pepper.

3. Drain the tagliatelle and quickly return to the pan. Immediately add the cheese mixture and toss it through the pasta using 2 forks. If liked, put the pan over a *very* low heat for a minute or two, shaking and tossing the pan.

4. Serve straight away.

CREAMY PASTA WITH BROCCOLI AND HAM

•

—— SERVES 2–3 ——

THIS recipe uses the same method as Herb and Pecorino or Parmesan Carbonara (see opposite) so it is important to work quickly after the ingredients have been brought together, or to reheat them *very* gently. The sauce that bathes the pasta and broccoli is made extra creamy by the addition of soft cheese.

225g (½lb) pasta shells
225g (½lb) broccoli florets
50g (2oz) Parma ham
3 eggs, at room temperature

25g (1oz) soft cheese
salt and freshly ground black pepper
freshly grated Parmesan cheese to
serve

1. Bring a large and a medium-sized saucepan of salted water to the boil. Add the pasta to the large pan, stir, then cover the pan and quickly return to the boil. Remove the lid and cook according to the instructions on the pack until tender but still firm to the bite. Cook the broccoli in the medium-sized saucepan, timing it to be ready at the same time as the pasta.

2. Meanwhile, chop the ham, then beat with the eggs and pepper.

3. Quickly drain the broccoli and the pasta and put into the pan in which the pasta was cooked. Immediately stir in the egg and ham mixture and the soft cheese. If the sauce does not begin to thicken, put the pan over a very low heat and shake and toss the pan until the sauce does show signs of thickening. Serve immediately with freshly grated Parmesan.

PASTA WITH BROCCOLI AND GORGONZOLA CHEESE

•

—— SERVES 4 ——

INSTEAD of milk you could use 4 tablespoons single or whipping cream, or 175ml (6fl oz) medium-bodied dry white wine boiled until it is reduced by half.

350g (12oz) broccoli
350g (12oz) pasta shells
175g (6oz) Gorgonzola cheese
4 tablespoons milk

a small knob of unsalted butter
40g (1½oz) walnut halves, chopped
freshly ground black pepper

1. Bring 2 large saucepans of salted water to the boil.

2. Meanwhile, divide the broccoli into florets. Trim the stalks and slice thinly diagonally. Add to one of the pans, cover and return quickly to the boil. Boil until tender.

3. Add the pasta to the other pan of water, stir, then cover the pan and quickly return to the boil. Remove the lid and cook according to the instructions on the pack until tender but still firm to the bite. Time it to be ready at the same time as the broccoli.

4. While the broccoli and pasta are cooking, chop the cheese and heat gently with the milk and butter, stirring until smooth; do not allow to boil. Season with pepper.

5. Drain the broccoli and the pasta, then toss together with the cheese sauce and walnuts.

FUSILLI WITH TOMATOES, COURGETTES AND MOZZARELLA CHEESE

•

—— SERVES 4 ——

ALTHOUGH all the ingredients are available throughout the year I always feel that this is a summer pasta dish – not only because it is light and fresh tasting but because the courgettes, tomatoes and herbs are at their best then.

2 medium courgettes
4 tablespoons virgin olive oil
350g (12oz) fusilli
2 small cloves garlic, crushed
1 × 150g (5oz) mozzarella cheese

2 well-flavoured tomatoes
2 teaspoons chopped parsley
1 tablespoon chopped basil
juice of $\frac{1}{2}$ lemon
salt and freshly ground black pepper

1. Bring a saucepan of salted water to the boil.

2. Meanwhile, thinly slice the courgettes and heat 2 tablespoons of the oil in a frying pan.

3. Add the fusilli to the water, stir, then cover the pan and quickly return to the boil. Remove the lid and cook for 4–5 minutes if fresh, 8–9 minutes if dried, until tender but still firm to the bite.

4. Add the courgettes to the frying pan and fry for about 4–5 minutes until tender, adding the garlic towards the end.

5. Chop the cheese and the tomatoes and add the tomatoes to the courgettes for the last 2 minutes or so of cooking so that they warm through.

6. Drain the fusilli and toss with the cheese, herbs, lemon juice, courgettes and tomatoes and the remaining oil. Season and serve.

SPAGHETTI WITH GOAT'S CHEESE PANCETTA, WALNUTS AND TOMATOES

•

—— SERVES 4 ——

THIS is quite a substantial pasta dish so it is suitable for a light meal, possibly followed by a simple salad, or it could be served as a main course. You can use soft, medium or firm goat's cheese, or goat's cheese that has been kept in oil, depending on what you like.

3 tablespoons olive oil
225g ($\frac{1}{2}$lb) pancetta or smoked
  bacon, chopped
1 clove garlic
75g (3oz) walnuts
$\frac{1}{2}$ onion

450g (1lb) well-flavoured tomatoes
225g ($\frac{1}{2}$lb) soft goat's cheese
350g (12oz) spaghetti
grated zest of 1 lemon
4 tablespoons chopped parsley
freshly ground black pepper

1. Bring a large saucepan of salted water to the boil. Heat the oil in a frying pan, then add the pancetta or bacon and start to fry it.

2. Crush the garlic, coarsely chop the walnuts and chop the onion. Add to the pancetta or bacon and fry until the garlic, walnuts and onion are golden.

3. Meanwhile, seed and chop the tomatoes and chop the cheese.

4. Add the spaghetti to the boiling water, stir, then cover the pan and return quickly to the boil. Remove the lid and cook for 3–4 minutes if fresh, about 8 minutes if dried, until tender but still firm to the bite.

5. Add the tomatoes, lemon zest, parsley and pepper to the frying pan and heat gently for a couple of minutes to warm through.

6. Drain the spaghetti and toss with the tomato mixture and the cheese. Serve straight away.

PASTA WITH SCALLOPS AND RED PESTO

•

—— SERVES 4 ——

THIS recipe fits the bill when I want something that will be impressive and taste special but have only a very short time in which to prepare and cook it. An additional advantage is that it uses mainly store-cupboard ingredients.

2 cloves garlic
1 shallot or ½ smallish onion, coarsely
  chopped
40g (1½oz) basil leaves
4 drained sun-dried tomato halves in
  oil, coarsely chopped
2 tablespoons oil from the tomatoes
7 tablespoons extra virgin olive oil
25g (1oz) walnut halves

2 tablespoons pine nuts or almond
  halves
5 tablespoons freshly grated
  Parmesan cheese
450g (1lb) shelled small scallops
400g (14oz) pappardelle or other
  ribbon noodles
salt and freshly ground black pepper

1. Bring a large saucepan of salted water to the boil.

2. Meanwhile, with the motor running, drop the garlic into a blender and process until coarsely chopped. Add the shallot or onion, basil, sun-dried tomato halves, sun-dried tomato oil, 5 tablespoons of the olive oil and the nuts. Mix until fairly smooth. Scoop into a bowl and stir in the cheese and plenty of pepper but only a little salt. Set this red pesto aside.

3. Heat the remaining oil in a large, preferably non-stick frying pan. Chop 115g (4oz) of the scallops. Add the whole scallops to the pan and fry, stirring frequently, for 3–4 minutes until just translucent; add the chopped scallops about 1 minute before the whole scallops are ready. Remove the pan from the heat.

4. While the scallops are cooking, add the pasta to the boiling water, stir, then cover the pan and quickly return to the boil. Remove the lid and cook according to the instructions on the pack until tender but still firm to the bite.

5. Drain the pasta, and toss with the scallops and red pesto.

PASTA WITH TUNA

•

—— SERVES 4 ——

THE sauce can be made more gutsy by using the red pepper and mashing four chopped anchovy fillets into the pan with it so that they dissolve. Use 3 tomatoes if you include the red pepper, 4 tomatoes if you leave it out. For a treat, you could use 450g (1lb) diced fresh tuna; fry it until lightly browned and just cooked through.

2 tablespoons virgin olive oil
1 clove garlic, cut into fine slivers
1 red pepper, grilled and peeled if liked (see opposite), chopped or sliced (optional)
1 × 200g (7oz) can tuna in oil or brine
3 or 4 well-flavoured tomatoes, depending on whether the red pepper is used

50g (2oz) black olives, preferably oil-cured, stones removed
300g (10oz) penne or other short tubes, or pasta shapes
leaves from a large sprig of basil, chopped
salt and freshly ground black pepper

1. Bring a large saucepan of salted water to the boil. Heat the oil in a frying pan and add the garlic, and red pepper, if used. If the pepper has not been grilled and peeled, cook it until it begins to soften.

2. Meanwhile, drain and flake the tuna, seed and chop the tomatoes and slice the olives lengthways. Add the pasta to the boiling water, stir, then cover the pan and return quickly to the boil. Remove the lid and cook according to the instructions on the pack until tender but still firm to the bite.

3. Add the tomatoes, tuna, olives, basil leaves and seasoning to the frying pan and cook gently for about 2 minutes. Add the grilled red pepper, if used.

4. Drain the pasta and return to the pan. Toss in the sauce and serve.

PASTA WITH RED PEPPERS AND SMOKED TROUT

•

SERVES 4

G RILLED peppers have an intriguing sweet-smoky taste that comp-lements the more pronounced smoky taste of smoked trout.

$2\frac{1}{2}$ large red peppers
400g (14oz) fettucine or other ribbon pasta
175–225g (6–8oz) smoked trout fillets

4 tablespoons virgin olive oil
4 tablespoons pine nuts
$2\frac{1}{2}$ tablespoons chopped basil
freshly ground black pepper

1. Preheat the grill. Halve the red peppers, then grill until charred and blistered. Leave to cool slightly then, holding each pepper half in turn over a bowl, remove the skin. Thinly slice the peppers.

2. Meanwhile, bring a large saucepan of salted water to the boil. Add the pasta, stir, then cover the pan and quickly return to the boil. Remove the lid and cook according to the instructions on the pack until tender but still firm to the bite.

3. While the pasta is cooking, flake the smoked trout and heat the oil in a large saucepan.

4. Add the pepper strips and any reserved juice and the pine nuts to the oil. Heat gently for 1 minute, then add the smoked trout. Cover and remove from the heat.

5. Drain the pasta, then add to the pan with the peppers and trout. Add the basil and pepper. Toss to mix, then serve.

PASTA WITH SAUSAGES AND TOMATO SAUCE

•

—— SERVES 3–4 ——

THIS is a favourite recipe for when I have walked with the dog for longer than I intended, or when I am in the middle of a hard day's gardening and want something quick, tasty and sustaining.

2 tablespoons olive oil
1 onion, sliced
2 cloves garlic, crushed
350–450g (12–16oz) coarse fresh
  spicy Italian sausages
300ml (½ pint) passata

350g (12oz) dried shell or similar
  pasta
2–3 tablespoons chopped parsley
salt and freshly ground black pepper
freshly grated Parmesan cheese to
  serve

1. Heat the oil in a frying pan and fry the onion and garlic until soft.

2. Meanwhile, bring a large saucepan of salted water to the boil. Remove the skin from the sausages and chop them into large pieces. Add to the onion and cook over a high heat, stirring, until browned.

3. Stir in the passata, bring to the boil, then cover and simmer for about 15 minutes.

4. While the sauce is cooking, add the pasta to the boiling water, stir, then cover the pan and return quickly to the boil. Remove the lid and cook according to the instructions on the pack until tender but still firm to the bite.

5. Stir the parsley and seasoning into the sauce.

6. Drain the pasta and pour into a warm serving bowl. Pour the sauce over the pasta and toss lightly. Serve with freshly grated Parmesan.

—— **VARIATION** ——

For Pasta with Salami and Tomato Sauce, omit the fresh sausages. Instead, add about 175g (6oz) chopped salami at Step 3. If liked, a chopped red chilli can be fried with the onion and garlic, or a dash of chilli sauce added at Step 3.

Pizza with Tomatoes and Garlic

•

—— SERVES 2 ——

THIS is a pizza to eat with a knife and fork, not in your fingers, as you will need to mash the garlic cloves while you eat the pizza. Instead of using a ready-made pizza base, you could made up a 145g (5oz) packet of pizza base mix (or, when you have plenty of time, make your own pizza base) and work in about 1½ tablespoons chopped mixed herbs.

4 well-flavoured tomatoes
1 bulb of garlic
1½–2 tablespoons virgin olive oil
75g (3oz) mozzarella cheese
1 x 25cm (10 inch) ready-made pizza
   base or 1 x 145g (5oz) pack pizza
   base mix

flour
about 8 black olives, preferably oil-
   cured
leaves from a small sprig of
   rosemary, chopped
salt and freshly ground black pepper
fresh basil leaves to garnish

1. Preheat the oven according to the instructions on the pizza base pack.

2. Chop the tomatoes, put into a bowl and mix with about 1 teaspoon salt; set aside.

3. Divide the garlic into cloves and mix with 1½–2 tablespoons oil.

4. Chop the cheese.

5. If using a packet of pizza base mix, make it according to the instructions on the packet and roll it out to a 25cm (10 inch) diameter circle. Put the pizza base on a lightly floured baking sheet.

6. Spoon the tomatoes on to the pizza base and scatter the garlic cloves, olives, rosemary and cheese over them.

7. Bake for about 20 minutes or according to the instructions on the pack. Season with plenty of pepper and garnish with basil leaves.

Aubergine, Salami and Goat's Cheese Pizza

•

INSTEAD of using chopped herbs to flavour the passata you could replace them with 4–5 tablespoons pesto. Alternatively, substitute about 6 tablespoons drained canned chopped tomatoes with herbs for the passata.

1 small aubergine, about 175g (6oz)
150g (5oz) salami
about 6 tablespoons passata
about 2 teaspoons chopped herbs
    such as parsley, basil or thyme
2 ready-made pizza bases, each
    about 20cm (8 inches) in diameter

150g (5oz) goat's cheese
about 8 black olives, preferably oil-
    cured
about 8 basil leaves, coarsely
    shredded
salt and freshly ground black pepper

1. Preheat the oven according to the instructions on the pizza base packs.

2. Thinly slice the aubergine and salami.

3. Mix the passata with the herbs and seasoning, then spread over the pizza bases. Cover with the aubergines and salami slices, interleaving them with each other. Crumble the goat's cheese over the slices and scatter the olives over them.

4. Grind pepper over the pizzas and bake for about 20 minutes or according to the instructions on the pack. Sprinkle with the basil a few minutes before the end of cooking.

—— • ——

Fish

Fɪsʜ is an ideal food for cooking quickly and also meets the trend towards a light, healthy diet. Portions and fillets cook more quickly than whole fish – as well as appealing to people who are put off fish by the bones – but their quality deteriorates quickly, so always try to buy ones that have been prepared specially for you. Italy's long coastline means that fish and shellfish feature prominently in Italian diets, especially near the coast. Inland, from central Italy northwards, streams that tumble down from the mountains provide freshwater fish such as trout.

Unfortunately, many varieties of fish, and particularly shellfish and crustaceans, from the Adriatic and Mediterranean seas are difficult, impossible or expensive to find outside Italy and southern Europe. So for some recipes I have used more readily available ones that lend themselves to Italian recipes.

BREAM WITH LEMON AND MARJORAM

•

S EVERAL varieties of sea bream are found around the Italian coast –
dentex, gilthead, bogue and black-banded. The first two are generally
considered to have superior eating qualities. Fortunately, both are becoming more readily available in Britain. They are ideally suited to this light,
simple recipe but you could use small sea bass or hake instead or, at a
pinch, trout.

50g (2oz) unsalted butter, diced
4 sea bream, each weighing about
   350g (12oz)
3 cloves garlic, lightly crushed

1 teaspoon chopped marjoram
1 tablespoon lemon juice
salt and freshly ground black pepper
lemon wedges to serve

1. Melt the butter in a frying pan large enough to hold the fish in a single
layer. Add the fish, garlic and marjoram and cook for 4 minutes, turning
the fish halfway through.

2. Add the lemon juice and pepper, cover the pan and cook for 10–12
minutes, turning the fish again halfway through.

3. Season the fish and transfer to a warm serving plate. Pour the cooking
juices over them and serve with lemon wedges.

FISH WITH COURGETTES

•

Hake is the common Mediterranean white fish. After a period of being out of favour it is beginning to grow in popularity once more in Britain. It has a fairly soft, white flesh and delicate flavour. If you are unable to find it or would prefer cod or halibut, either of these can be used instead.

2 hake, cod or halibut steaks, each
  weighing 150–175g (5–6oz)
2 tablespoons olive oil, plus extra for
  brushing
½ small red onion, finely chopped
1 clove garlic, chopped
115ml (4fl oz) fish stock
115ml (4fl oz) medium-bodied dry
  white wine

250g (9oz) small courgettes
1 tomato
3 anchovy fillets
1 tablespoon chopped basil and
  parsley
salt and freshly ground black pepper

1. Preheat the grill. Season the fish and brush lightly with oil. Grill for about 5 minutes a side depending on thickness, until the flesh flakes when tested with a fork.

2. Meanwhile, heat the oil in a frying pan or a wide saucepan. Add the onion and garlic and fry until soft but not coloured. Add the stock and wine, then boil until reduced to about one-third (6 tablespoons). Add the courgettes and cook until they are just tender but still retain some bite.

3. Seed and chop the tomato and chop the anchovies. Add to the cooked courgettes with the herbs and seasoning. Heat for about 1 minute.

4. Transfer the courgette mixture to two warmed plates and put the fish on top.

FRIED COD WITH WARM GREEN SALSA
•

—— SERVES 4 ——

THE flavoured sauce goes well with the firm, large flakes of cod to make a dish that tastes satisfying yet is neither rich nor heavy.

1 tablespoon olive oil
4 cod cutlets or steaks, preferably
  fresh, each weighing 150–175g
  (5–6oz)
2 anchovy fillets
3 cloves garlic
1 tablespoon chopped basil
2 tablespoons chopped parsley

1½ tablespoons capers
1¼ teaspoons wholegrain mustard
4 tablespoons lemon juice
2 tablespoons virgin or extra virgin
  olive oil
freshly ground black pepper

1. Heat the olive oil in a non-stick frying pan, then add the cod and cook for about 5 minutes a side until the flesh flakes easily when tested with a fork.

2. Meanwhile, finely chop the anchovy fillets and crush with the garlic and basil to make a paste. Mix in the parsley, capers, mustard, lemon juice, oil and pepper.

3. Pour the sauce around the fish and warm through briefly.

4. Remove the fish from the frying pan and serve with the sauce poured over.

FISH WITH EGG, PARMESAN AND BASIL SAUCE

•

—— SERVES 4 ——

IF THIS dish is planned ahead, or you are able to start preparing it in advance, you can save time at the last minute by making the sauce – or at least boiling the eggs. Don't leave the eggs to cool in the water in which they have been boiled. If you do, there will be unsightly grey-black rings around the yolks.

2 large eggs at room temperature
8 brill or lemon sole fillets, each weighing about 150g (5oz)
virgin olive oil
leaves from 1½ large handfuls of basil

1 plump clove garlic
75g (3oz) freshly grated Parmesan cheese
salt and freshly ground black pepper

1. Bring a small saucepan of water to the boil, then add the eggs and simmer for 8–10 minutes, depending on whether you want the yolks still slightly creamy or hard.

2. Meanwhile, preheat the grill. Season the fish and lightly flatten with the back of a knife. Fold each one in half, brush with oil and grill for 8–10 minutes, turning the fish halfway through.

3. Finely chop the basil leaves and garlic.

4. Drain the eggs and rinse under running cold water until cool enough to peel. Peel and chop the eggs, then mix with the basil, garlic and cheese. Beat in enough oil to make a soft sauce that will hold its shape. Season with plenty of pepper – salt may not be necessary because of the cheese.

5. Serve the sauce with the fish.

FISH WITH POLENTA CRUST AND BASIL AND OLIVE VINAIGRETTE

•

———— SERVES 4 ————

COARSE polenta makes a delicious, crisp coating that keeps the fish succulent during cooking. Should you feel the sauce needs more distinction, add some sun-dried tomato paste or a dash of balsamic vinegar.

coarse polenta for coating
4 skinned fish fillets, each weighing
   150–175g (5–6oz)
1 egg, beaten
olive oil and unsalted butter for frying
salt and freshly ground black pepper

BASIL AND OLIVE VINAIGRETTE
1 plump clove garlic
115ml (4fl oz) extra virgin olive oil

$1\frac{1}{2}$ tablespoons red wine vinegar
1 tablespoon chopped basil or
   parsley
225g ($\frac{1}{2}$lb) well-flavoured tomatoes,
   seeded and finely chopped
65g ($2\frac{1}{2}$oz) pitted black olives,
   preferably oil-cured, chopped
salt and freshly ground black pepper

1. Season the polenta, then put a thick layer on a plate.

2. Season the fish, dip in the beaten egg and allow the excess egg to drain off. Press into the polenta, then turn over and press in the other side to coat lightly, evenly and firmly.

3. Heat a shallow layer of oil and butter in a frying pan. Add the fish and cook for about 3 minutes a side.

4. Meanwhile, make the vinaigrette: Crush the garlic with a pinch of salt, then mix with the oil, vinegar and basil or parsley. Finally, add the tomatoes, olives and pepper.

5. Serve the fish with the vinaigrette.

SKATE WITH CAPER VINAIGRETTE

•

—— SERVES 2 ——

THE piquant vinaigrette is made while the skate is cooking so the complete dish is very quickly ready to eat.

15g (½oz) butter
2 tablespoons olive oil
2 skate wings, each weighing about
    225g (½lb)
1 well-flavoured tomato
1 heaped teaspoon capers
½ small red onion or 1 small shallot or
    ¼ onion

1½ teaspoons chopped parsley
1 teaspoon chopped basil
2 tablespoons white wine vinegar
4 tablespoons virgin olive oil
salt and freshly ground black pepper

1. Heat the butter and oil in a wide frying pan. Season the skate, add to the pan and cook until lightly browned on both sides.

2. Meanwhile, seed and chop the tomato, coarsely chop the capers and finely chop the onion or shallot. Mix with the herbs, oil and pepper.

3. Transfer the skate to warm plates and serve with the sauce poured over them.

MACKEREL WITH OLIVES AND TOMATOES

•

—— SERVES 4 ——

THE tomatoes are not cooked down to a sauce but are given the briefest of heatings with the olives, garlic and herbs so that they are warm and still retain their shape. The heat brings out the flavour of the ingredients to make a kind of warm, fragrant relish.

1 tablespoon olive oil
4 mackerel fillets, each weighing
*   about 115g (4oz)*
1 clove garlic
4 ripe but firm well-flavoured
*   tomatoes*
8 pitted black olives

25g (1oz) unsalted butter
juice of $\frac{1}{2}$ lemon
1 tablespoon chopped parsley
1 teaspoon chopped thyme leaves
salt and freshly ground black pepper

1. Heat the oil in a non-stick frying pan. With the point of a sharp knife, cut 2 or 3 slashes in the skin of each fillet. Add to the pan, skin-side down, and fry until golden. Turn the fillets over and fry on the other side. Using a fish slice, transfer the fish to a warm plate, season and keep warm.

2. Meanwhile, crush the garlic, seed and chop the tomatoes and slice the olives.

3. Add the butter to the pan. When it is foaming, add the garlic, tomatoes and olives. Heat for a minute or so, shaking the pan. Add the lemon juice, herbs and seasoning and pour over the fish.

TROTA DEL NERA

•

THE River Nera in Umbria, one of seven land-locked Italian provinces, was traditionally the source of wild trout. They had such a fine flavour and succulent flesh that they were cooked and served quite plainly to highlight their quality. Nowadays, as elsewhere, farmed trout are widely available. These less distinguished fish need more help if they are to make memorable dishes – this modern recipe adds a vibrant salad.

4 trout, each weighing about 300g (10oz)
175ml (6fl oz) virgin olive oil, plus extra for brushing
1 lemon, halved
$\frac{1}{2}$ red onion
1 clove garlic
10 capers, preferably salt-packed

16 oil-cured black olives, stoned
4 halves sun-dried tomatoes
1 tablespoon red wine vinegar
leaves from a very large bunch of flat-leaved parsley
salt and freshly ground black pepper
plump lemon wedges to serve

1. Preheat the grill. With the point of a sharp knife, cut 3 slashes in each side of every trout. Brush the trout inside and out with olive oil, squeeze lemon juice over them and grill for 5–7 minutes a side depending on thickness.

2. Meanwhile, coarsely chop the onion, then add the garlic, capers, olives and sun-dried tomatoes and chop them together. Put into a bowl and stir in the vinegar and oil.

3. Add the parsley and seasoning to the salad and serve with the fish, accompanied by lemon wedges.

GRILLED SALMON WITH TOMATOES AND BASIL

•

——— SERVES 2 ———

SOME sliced, pitted black olives can be added to the tomato and parsley mixture, if liked.

3 tablespoons virgin olive oil, plus
   extra for brushing
20g (⅔oz) basil leaves
2 salmon steaks, each weighing
   about 175g (6oz)

2 large well-flavoured tomatoes
1 tablespoon chopped parsley
salt and freshly ground black pepper

1. Preheat the grill. Mix the oil and basil in a blender until smooth. Season and set aside.

2. Season the salmon and brush with oil. Grill for about 4 minutes a side.

3. Meanwhile, chop the tomatoes; discard the seeds, if liked. Mix the tomatoes with the parsley and seasoning. Divide between 2 plates.

4. Add the salmon steaks to the plate and trickle basil oil over each steak.

SICILIAN TUNA

•

Tuna fisheries have existed in southern Italy for centuries and were of major commercial importance, but now they are declining along with the size of the catch. Sicily is one place where there are still a number of fisheries and this is a favourite Sicilian way of cooking tuna.

4 tablespoons olive oil
2 large onions, thinly sliced
4 tuna steaks, each weighing 175–
    200g (6–7oz) and 2cm (¾ inch)
    thick
1 tablespoon brown sugar

3 tablespoons red wine vinegar
75ml (3fl oz) dry white wine
salt and freshly ground black pepper
chopped parsley to serve

1. Heat 3 tablespoons of the oil in a large frying pan, then add the onions and fry until soft. Increase the heat and continue to cook until the onions are a rich golden-brown. Using a slotted spoon, remove and reserve them.

2. Add the remaining oil to the pan. When it is hot, add the tuna and fry briskly until browned on both sides. Lower the heat for 1 minute before stirring in the sugar, vinegar and wine.

3. Return the onions to the pan to surround the tuna. Season, cover and cook over a high heat for 2 minutes.

4. Serve sprinkled with parsley.

SWORDFISH WITH SALMORIGLIO

•

——— SERVES 4 ———

SALMORIGLIO is a mixture of olive oil and herbs and throughout Sicily it is brushed on fish steaks or pieces of fish threaded on skewers before they are grilled (preferably over a barbecue). The remaining dressing is served separately with the fish. Sicilians believe the only way to make salmoriglio is to add sea water; in my kitchen I make the nearest replica I can by using sea salt. Tuna can be used instead of swordfish.

1 small clove garlic
2 teaspoons finely chopped parsley
$\frac{1}{4}$ teaspoon dried oregano
$\frac{3}{4}$ teaspoon finely chopped rosemary
juice of 1 small lemon

115ml (4fl oz) virgin olive oil
4 swordfish steaks, each weighing
  about 175g (6oz)
sea salt and freshly ground black
  pepper

1. Crush the garlic with a pinch of sea salt then, using a fork, whisk with the herbs and lemon juice. Still whisking, slowly pour in the oil then 2 tablespoons hot water to make a thick sauce. Season with pepper.

2. Either leave the fish steaks whole or cut them into cubes; thread the cubes on to skewers. Lay the steaks or skewers in a shallow, non-metallic dish. Pour the sauce over, turn the steaks or skewers over, then leave for 30–45 minutes, turning occasionally. (Whole steaks can, if liked, be left for up to 1 hour.)

3. Preheat the grill to fairly hot.

4. Grill skewers for 6–7 minutes, turning occasionally, steaks for about 4 minutes a side, until the flesh flakes when tested with a fork; brush with the dressing when turning the skewers or fish. Serve the remaining dressing with the fish.

GRILLED SARDINES IN VINE LEAVES

•

—— SERVES 4 ——

THE aroma of sardines cooking over a barbecue, perhaps by the sea so that there is an enhancing sea-salt tang in the air, is one of the most evocative there is. This is a good way of cooking sardines when you do not have time to leave them to marinate, because the vine leaves lend a piquant taste. If you do not have vine leaves you can brush the sardines with the garlic, parsley and lemon mixture before and during cooking.

12 fresh or preserved vine leaves
12 fresh sardines, cleaned
2 cloves garlic

leaves from a large bunch of parsley
finely grated zest and juice of 1 lemon
salt and freshly ground black pepper

1. Preheat the grill. If using preserved vine leaves, rinse them well under running hot water. Season the sardines then wrap each one in a vine leaf.

2. Grill the sardines for about 3–4 minutes a side.

3. Meanwhile, chop the garlic and parsley together very finely. Mix with the lemon zest and juice and seasoning.

4. Serve the garlic and parsley mixture separately, to be eaten with each mouthful of sardine.

SARDINES WITH OLIVE OIL, LEMON AND OREGANO

•

—— SERVES 2 ——

OREGANO is the herb that speaks most strongly of southern Italian cooking; low bushes decked with white or pale pink flowers in summer can be seen growing wild on the hillsides throughout the south. Bunches, flowers and all, are hung to dry in the warm sunshine because this is the one herb whose flavour develops when it is dried. It is slightly minty and goes particularly well with oily fish such as sardines.

350–450g (12–16oz) fresh sardines, cleaned
2–3 tablespoons virgin olive oil
1½ tablespoons lemon juice

1½ teaspoons dried oregano
salt and freshly ground black pepper
lemon wedges to serve

1. Lay the sardines in a shallow, non-metallic dish. Pour the olive oil and lemon juice over them, sprinkle with half the oregano and season. Turn the fish over, sprinkle with the remaining oregano and season. Leave for 10–30 minutes.

2. Preheat the grill.

3. Grill the sardines for 5–10 minutes depending on size, turning them once or twice and brushing with the marinade as they are turned. Serve with lemon wedges.

RED MULLET WITH PARMA HAM AND BASIL OR SAGE

•

SERVES 2–4

IF preferred two whole red mullet can be used instead of fillets; put the sage or basil leaves in the cavity of the fish and cook for about 5 minutes a side, depending on size.

4 red mullet fillets, each weighing
   75–115g (3–4oz)
4 sage leaves or large basil leaves
4 large slices of Parma ham

olive oil
freshly ground black pepper
$\frac{1}{2}$ lemon

1. Season each red mullet fillet with pepper, place a sage or basil leaf on top, then wrap in a slice of Parma ham.

2. Heat a thin layer of oil in a large frying pan. Add the fish and cook gently for about 3 minutes until the ham is crisp. Turn the fish over and fry on the other side for 2 minutes.

3. Transfer the fish to warm plates and squeeze lemon juice over them.

GRILLED SQUID WITH PARSLEY, GARLIC AND CHILLI RELISH

•

—— SERVES 4 ——

THERE is no need to chew through rubbery squid when you use small ones and cook them quickly. (Large squid are best cooked gently for a long time to make sure they are tender; beating with a meat bat or rolling pin also helps.) Prepared squid are available from supermarkets.

6 fresh red chillies
4 cloves garlic
leaves and fine stems from ½ bunch
    of parsley

8–10 prepared small squid
2–3 tablespoons extra virgin olive oil
salt and freshly ground black pepper
lemon wedges to serve

1. Remove the seeds from the chillies. Chop the chillies finely; reserve 1 tablespoonful. Finely chop the remaining chillies with the garlic and parsley.

2. Slit the squid bodies lengthways in half and score the undersides of each half. Toss with the reserved chilli and the oil and seasoning. Leave for up to 30–45 minutes.

3. Preheat the grill to very hot. Grill the squid, scored side down first, for 2 minutes each side until tender.

4. Serve the squid with the parsley, garlic and chilli relish and accompany with lemon wedges.

GRILLED SCALLOPS WITH HERBS AND LEMON

•

—— SERVES 2 ——

I F YOU do not have any skewers the scallops can be put on the grill rack, but they will be more fiddly to turn over. Chunks of fresh firm, white fish such as cod, halibut or monkfish can also be prepared in the same way.

450g (1lb) shelled scallops
bay leaves
3 tablespoons extra virgin olive oil
1½ tablespoons lemon juice

2 teaspoons mixed chopped herbs
* such as oregano, basil, parsley,*
* fennel and chives*
salt and freshly ground black pepper

1. Thread the scallops on to skewers, alternating with bay leaves. Lay the skewers in a shallow dish.

2. Mix together the oil, lemon juice, herbs and seasoning. Pour the dressing over the scallops, turn them over and set aside for 30 minutes or at least while the grill is heating.

3. Preheat the grill.

4. Grill the scallops for 4–5 minutes, turning occasionally and brushing with the remaining oil mixture as the skewers are turned.

ABRUZZESE PRAWNS WITH 'HOT' TOMATO SAUCE

•

—— SERVES 3 – 4 ——

CHILLIES are used in southern Italian cooking. They are the local spice of Abruzzo, where they are called *diavolicchio* (little devil), and the one most commonly used there; a dish described as *all'abruzzese* (in the style of Abruzzo) will be generously flavoured with them. (The amount of chilli in this dish is more restrained.)

3 tablespoons virgin olive oil
1 red onion, finely chopped
1 plump clove garlic
450g (1lb) well-flavoured tomatoes, or 350g (12oz) canned chopped tomatoes

$\frac{1}{2}$ small dried red chilli
2 tablespoons chopped parsley
550g (1$\frac{1}{4}$lb) large prawns in their shells
salt

1. Heat the oil, add the onion and cook until soft but not coloured.

2. Meanwhile, chop the garlic and tomatoes; the tomatoes can be peeled if liked.

3. Add the garlic to the onion, crumble in the chilli and cook until the garlic is lightly coloured.

4. Stir in the parsley, then add the tomatoes. Bring to the boil, then simmer steadily, uncovered, for 15–20 minutes, stirring occasionally.

5. While the sauce is cooking, peel the prawns. Add them to the sauce, turn them over and cook through for about 4 minutes, stirring occasionally. Season the sauce with salt to taste and serve.

Prawns with Chilli and Garlic

•

—— SERVES 2 ——

THIS is a dish to serve to family or good friends, or people you know will not mind abandoning knives and forks in favour of fingers. This is because the best way to eat the prawns is with your fingers; you take off the prawn heads and suck the flesh from the body shells – delicious but messy. You then mop up the juices, richly flavoured by the prawns, chilli and garlic, with good bread.

2 tablespoons olive oil
50g (2oz) unsalted butter, diced
3 plump cloves garlic, crushed
1 dried red chilli, seeded and
  chopped

12 uncooked large (Mediterranean)
  prawns in their shells
1 large lemon, halved
salt

1. Heat the oil and butter in a large, heavy frying pan, add the garlic, chilli and prawns and fry over a high heat, shaking and tossing the pan constantly.

2. Squeeze in the juice from one half of the lemon, add salt and serve immediately with the remaining lemon-half cut into halves.

BUTTERFLIED PRAWNS

•

THE prawns take only 3 minutes to cook but they do benefit from marinating for up to 30 minutes, so, if possible, put them in the marinade before you prepare the rest of the meal, even if that only involves making a salad to accompany the prawns, laying the table and perhaps relaxing with a drink.

*450g (1lb) jumbo prawns in their
  shells*
½ clove garlic, crushed
5 tablespoons virgin olive oil
4 tablespoons lemon juice

*2 tablespoons sun-dried tomato
  paste*
1 tablespoon chopped basil
a small dash of chilli sauce
salt and freshly ground black pepper

1. Remove the heads and legs from the prawns. Using sharp scissors, cut the prawns almost in half lengthways, leaving the tails intact. Put in a shallow dish and add the garlic, 2 tablespoons of the oil and 2 tablespoons of the lemon juice. Stir together. Leave for up to 30 minutes, if possible.

2. Preheat the grill. Stir together the remaining oil and lemon juice and the tomato paste, basil, chilli sauce and seasoning.

3. Grill the prawns for about 3 minutes until they turn bright pink and have 'butterflied'. Serve them with the tomato and chilli sauce spooned over, or serve the sauce in a small bowl as a dip.

CHAPTER FIVE

Poultry & Meat

Iᴛᴀʟɪᴀɴ chicken dishes have always found favour because they are invariably straightforward, simple and delicious. Chicken is also an obvious choice for the cook in a hurry as it is both quick cooking and versatile. The quality of the chicken will affect the quality of the dish so use a fresh, traditionally reared free-range bird. Corn-fed chickens have been fed a maize diet which colours their flesh yellow and gives it a richer, very slightly gamey taste that is more akin to how chicken used to taste.

Although Italy has never been a great meat-eating nation, grilling and frying, the two cooking methods most frequently used for meat, combined with typically Italian simple, bold flavours are custom-made for meals that have to be prepared in a hurry. You need to use lean cuts such as lamb chops, steaks and noisettes, pork steaks and escalopes, veal escalopes and beef sirloin and rump steaks for tender, quickly cooked meat.

Try to make sure that meat and poultry are at room temperature before you start to cook them; not only will they cook more quickly, they will also be more succulent. The timings in my recipes are for room-temperature meat and poultry so if you use colder products you will have to increase the cooking time.

PIQUANT CHICKEN WITH CAPERS

•

—— SERVES 4 ——

THE fresh, zingy flavours of capers and lemon zest and juice turn plain chicken breasts into a light, piquant dish.

1 tablespoon olive oil
25g (1oz) unsalted butter
4 chicken breast fillets, each
  weighing about 150g (5oz)

finely grated zest and juice of 1 lemon
1 tablespoon capers, preferably salt-
  packed
salt and freshly ground black pepper

1. Heat the oil and butter in a frying pan. Flatten the chicken breasts lightly with a meat mallet or the side of a large, heavy knife. Add to the pan, skin or skinned side down first, and fry gently for about 15 minutes until cooked and golden. Transfer to a warm plate, season and keep warm.

2. Stir the lemon zest and juice into the pan, dislodging the sediment, then add the capers and bring to the boil. Season and pour over the chicken.

CHICKEN WITH ROSEMARY AND LEMON

•

—— SERVES 4 ——

AFTER an initial browning with rosemary and garlic the chicken is cooked more gently with lemon juice and zest so that their flavour subtly impregnates its flesh.

1 tablespoon olive oil
25g (1oz) unsalted butter
1 sprig of rosemary
1 clove garlic

4 chicken breast fillets, each
  weighing about 150g (5oz)
juice and finely grated zest of 1 lemon
salt and freshly ground black pepper

1. Heat the oil, butter, rosemary and garlic in a frying pan and heat gently for 2–3 minutes.

2. Meanwhile, flatten the chicken breasts lightly with a meat mallet or the side of a large, heavy knife. Increase the heat beneath the pan, add the chicken, skin or skinned side down first, and fry for 3 minutes on each side.

3. Pour the lemon juice over the chicken, add the lemon zest and seasoning and cook over a medium heat, turning the chicken frequently, for about 10 minutes.

4. Discard the rosemary and garlic. Serve the chicken with the juices poured over.

SUMMER CHICKEN WITH BASIL

•

—— SERVES 4 ——

THIS is a beautiful dish to make in summer when fresh basil is at its most fragrant; it is then well worth buying good-quality, fresh, traditionally reared free-range chicken.

4 chicken breast fillets without skin,
  each weighing about 150g (5oz)
25g (1oz) unsalted butter
1 tablespoon olive oil

1 large juicy lemon
1½ handfuls of basil leaves
salt and freshly ground black pepper

1. Using a sharp knife, cut the chicken breasts in half horizontally. Beat with a meat mallet or the side of a large, heavy knife to flatten them slightly.

2. Heat the butter and oil in a large frying pan (the chicken must cook in a single layer). Add the chicken and fry for 3–4 minutes a side.

3. Meanwhile, squeeze the juice from the lemon and tear the basil leaves.

4. Pour the lemon juice over the chicken, then add the basil and seasoning. Turn the chicken over and cook gently for a couple of minutes or so.

5. Serve the chicken with the sauce spooned over.

Tuscan Chicken

•

—— SERVES 4 ——

This cooks gently for about 20 minutes so you have time to eat the first course or prepare a vegetable dish to accompany the chicken, or make a dessert. Then, just before serving, the ingredients for the sauce are quickly poured over the chicken and, almost instantly, it is ready. (In Liguria the sauce is cooked for longer to allow the eggs to be scrambled.) If liked, white wine can be substituted for some of the stock. Season with white pepper if you are a purist and feel that specks of black pepper would spoil the pure flavour and colour of the sauce; otherwise use black pepper. You may have to jiggle with the amount and cooking of the stock, adding more if it disappears too quickly, or turning up the heat if there is some left. Garnish as you like with fresh herbs such as marjoram, basil, chervil or thyme.

50g (2oz) butter
½ onion, very finely chopped
4 boneless chicken breasts, each weighing 150–175g (5–6oz)
about 225ml (8fl oz) chicken stock

1–1½ lemons
2 egg yolks
salt and freshly ground white or black pepper
chopped herbs to garnish (see above)

1. Melt the butter in a frying pan that will just hold the chicken in a single layer. Add the onion and cook until softened.

2. Add the chicken, skin or skinned side down first, and brown lightly on both sides.

3. Pour the stock over the chicken and heat to simmering point. Lower the heat and simmer gently, turning the chicken occasionally, for about 20 minutes, until it is tender and there is no stock left.

4. Meanwhile, squeeze the lemon or lemons to get 4 tablespoons juice. Mix the juice and seasoning with the egg yolks.

5. Remove the pan from the heat and immediately pour the lemon mixture over the chicken breasts, turning them quickly so that they are coated with the sauce; the heat of the chicken should set the egg to a light sauce but, if liked, you can cover the pan so that the egg heats for a little longer. Garnish with chopped herbs and serve.

CHICKEN WITH SAVOURY BASIL SAUCE

•

—— SERVES 4 ——

THE basil leaves inserted underneath the skin of the chicken breasts begin to flavour its flesh during cooking. This flavouring is enhanced by the savoury sauce (which is quickly and easily made while the chicken is cooking) which is eaten with the chicken in the same way as mustard, but in more generous amounts. The basil leaves can be inserted under the chicken skin ahead of time and the sauce can be made in advance.

leaves from a 50g (2oz) bunch of basil
4 chicken breast fillets with skin,
   each weighing about 150g (5oz)
1 clove garlic
4 teaspoons wholegrain mustard

4 tablespoons red wine vinegar
6 anchovy fillets
175ml (6fl oz) virgin olive oil
salt and freshly ground black pepper

1. Preheat the grill. Push 3 basil leaves under the skin of each chicken breast. Season the breasts and grill, skin-side up first, for 6–8 minutes a side.

2. Meanwhile, with the motor running, drop the garlic clove into a blender, then add the mustard, vinegar, anchovy fillets and remaining basil. When just mixed, slowly pour in the oil. Season with plenty of pepper.

3. Serve the chicken with the sauce.

CHICKEN BREAST PARCELS WITH DOLCELATTE

•

—— SERVES 2 ——

I FIND this a useful, and popular, recipe for when I am entertaining as it has a sophisticated Italian air, is richly flavoured but not heavily rich to eat and is easy to make and quick to cook. The preparation can be done ahead of time, even if only 30 or 60 minutes.

20g (¾oz) unsalted butter, diced
½ clove garlic, finely chopped
1 small shallot, finely chopped
2 chicken breast fillets without skin, each weighing about 150g (5oz)
about 1 teaspoon black olive paste

50g (2oz) piece of Dolcelatte, cut in half
4 sage or basil leaves
2 slices of Parma ham
6 tablespoons medium-bodied dry white wine
freshly ground black pepper

1. Heat the butter in a medium-sized frying pan, add the garlic and shallot and cook gently until beginning to soften.

2. Meanwhile, cut a deep lengthways pocket through the thick side of each chicken breast fillet. Spread black olive paste sparingly in each pocket and insert a piece of cheese. Place 2 sage or basil leaves on each breast, season with pepper, then wrap in a slice of Parma ham. Secure with wooden cocktail sticks or tie with string.

3. Using a slotted spoon, remove the shallot mixture from the pan and reserve.

4. Add the chicken to the pan and cook for about 2 minutes a side.

5. Return the shallot mixture to the pan, pour the wine over the chicken and bring to just on boiling point. Cover tightly and cook gently for about 12 minutes until the chicken is cooked through. Season with pepper.

6. Serve with the cooking juices spooned over.

CHICKEN, BREASTS WRAPPED IN SPINACH AND PARMA HAM

•

——— SERVES 2 ———

DON'T worry if you do not have quite enough chicken stock; simply make up the shortfall with water – or wine, if you like. The stock that is left after cooking the chicken is well flavoured and makes a good base for soups and casseroles.

2 large spinach leaves
2 boneless chicken breasts without
  skin, each weighing about 150g
  (5oz)
2 slices of Parma ham
about 350ml (12fl oz) chicken stock
3 tablespoons virgin olive oil

1 tablespoon walnut oil
1 tablespoon tarragon vinegar
$1\frac{1}{2}$ teaspoons chopped parsley
$1\frac{1}{2}$ tablespoons chopped dill
$\frac{1}{2}$ teaspoon wholegrain mustard
salt and freshly ground black pepper

1. Bring a saucepan of water to the boil. Remove the stalks from the spinach leaves and add the leaves to the boiling water. Cover and quickly return to the boil. Drain.

2. Season each chicken breast with black pepper and wrap in a slice of Parma ham, then in a spinach leaf.

3. Meanwhile, bring the stock to the boil in a saucepan that the chicken breasts will just fit into side by side. Add the chicken breasts to the pan; the loose end of each spinach leaf must be underneath. Cover and quickly return to the boil. Turn down the heat and poach for 18–20 minutes.

4. Mix the remaining ingredients, including seasoning, to a green purée in a blender.

5. Either serve the chicken on the sauce, or pour the sauce over the chicken.

CHICKEN WITH COURGETTE SAUCE

•

—— SERVES 4 ——

WHILE the flavour of virgin olive oil is an integral part of the sauce, quite a mild one should be used or the subtle flavour of the courgettes will be lost.

4 chicken breast fillets with skin, each weighing about 175g (6oz)
2 tablespoons olive oil
1 small onion, finely chopped
350g (12oz) small courgettes

2–3 tablespoons virgin olive oil
3 tablespoons chopped basil
2 teaspoons capers, preferably salt-packed, chopped
salt and freshly ground black pepper

1. Preheat the grill. Season the chicken breasts and grill, skin-side up first, for 6–8 minutes a side.

2. Meanwhile, heat the olive oil in a frying pan, add the onion and cook until beginning to soften.

3. While the onion is cooking, coarsely grate the courgettes. Add to the onion and add $1\frac{1}{2}$–2 tablespoons water. Cover and cook over a low heat, shaking the pan and stirring the courgettes frequently, for 8–10 minutes until the courgettes are tender.

4. Tip into a food processor, add the virgin olive oil and process to a nubbly purée. Return to the pan, add the basil, capers and seasoning and heat through.

5. Serve the chicken with the courgette sauce.

WARM CHICKEN AND COURGETTE SALAD

•

——— SERVES 4 ———

Black olives, capers and sun-dried tomatoes combine with chicken breasts and steamed courgettes to make a satisfying, lively yet light, salad for lunch or supper.

8 black olives, preferably oil-cured
1 tablespoon capers, preferably salt-
  packed
2 sun-dried tomatoes
1 small clove garlic
1½ tablespoons white wine vinegar
7 tablespoons virgin olive oil, plus
  extra for cooking

3 chicken breast fillets, with skin
225g (8oz) small courgettes
freshly ground black pepper
crisp lettuce leaves
small piece of Parmesan cheese to
  serve

1. Remove the stones from the olives if necessary. Chop the olives with the capers, sun-dried tomatoes and garlic. Mix with the vinegar and pepper, then whisk in the oil. Set aside.

2. Place each chicken breast in turn between 2 sheets of clingfilm and beat with a rolling pin to flatten thoroughly.

3. Heat a heavy, preferably non-stick, frying pan and brush with oil. Add the chicken breasts, skin-side down first, and fry for 3–4 minutes a side until brown and cooked through.

4. Meanwhile, bring a saucepan of water to the boil. Slice the courgettes lengthways, then lay them in a single layer, if possible, in a steaming basket, cover and steam for 4–5 minutes until tender.

5. Divide the lettuce leaves between 4 plates.

6. Cut the chicken breasts into wide strips and toss with the courgettes and dressing. Put on the lettuce leaves. Using a potato peeler, shave thin slices of Parmesan over the salad. Serve while warm.

ITALIAN WARM CHICKEN AND VEGETABLE SALAD

•

—— SERVES 4 ——

S KIN on the chicken breasts will help to prevent the flesh drying when they are grilled; if you do not want to eat the skin it can easily be discarded after cooking (it will not have added to the calorie content of the chicken). For quicker cooking, chicken breast fillets can be used; they should be brushed with oil before cooking.

3 tablespoons virgin olive oil
1 tablespoon walnut oil
1 tablespoon balsamic vinegar
salad leaves such as rocket, corn
   salad, frisée and Little Gem lettuce
1 bunch of chives
4 small chicken breasts, preferably
   with skin

175g (6oz) broccoli florets
175g (6oz) oyster, shiitake or brown
   cap mushrooms
$\frac{1}{2}$ fleshy red pepper
olive oil for frying
salt and freshly ground black pepper

1. Preheat the grill and bring a saucepan of water to the boil. Mix together the oils, vinegar and seasoning and put the salad leaves in a large salad bowl. Chop the chives.

2. Grill the chicken breasts, skin-side up first, for about 15 minutes, turning halfway through, until the juices run clear when the thickest part of the breast is pierced with a sharp knife.

3. Add the broccoli to the boiling water and cook until just tender.

4. Meanwhile, slice the mushrooms and chop the red pepper.

5. Heat the olive oil in a frying pan and fry the mushrooms and red pepper, stirring frequently so that they remain crisp.

6. Drain the broccoli very well. Slice the chicken breasts diagonally into strips. Remove the mushrooms and red pepper from the pan with a slotted spoon and toss with the broccoli, chicken, salad leaves and chives.

7. Stir the dressing into the frying pan and bring to the boil. Pour over the salad, toss lightly and serve.

PORK WITH SAGE

•

—— SERVES 4 ——

IF YOU have time, marinate the pork in the lemon juice for 30 minutes. Chicken or turkey fillets can be substituted for the pork.

1 tablespoon olive oil
50g (2oz) unsalted butter
4 slices of pork fillet, each weighing
  115–150g (4–5oz)

12 sage leaves, shredded
1 large thin-skinned lemon
salt and freshly ground black pepper

1. Heat the oil and about three-quarters of the butter in a frying pan. Season the pork with black pepper and add it to the pan with the sage. Fry until browned on both sides.

2. Meanwhile, squeeze the lemon – you need 4 tablespoons juice.

3. Transfer the pork to a warm plate, season and keep warm.

4. Pour most of the fat from the pan, leaving behind the sediment. Stir the lemon juice into the pan, dislodging the sediment, and bring to the boil. Lower the heat and stir in the remaining butter.

5. Return the pork to the pan and turn once or twice in the sauce before serving.

PORK WITH RED PEPPER AND GARLIC

•

—— SERVES 2 ——

I SOMETIMES start by putting the halved red pepper to grill then start to cook the rest of the dish. I add the pepper to the pork after peeling it (see page 63) so it only needs a few minutes to heat through. If you have red peppers preserved in vinegar, you can use about 200g (7oz) drained peppers instead of the fresh one. They just have to be heated through, and the wine can be omitted.

3 tablespoons olive oil
about 350g (12oz) pork fillet, cut into
  chunks
2–3 cloves garlic
1 fleshy red pepper

4 tablespoons medium-bodied dry
  white wine
a pinch of chilli flakes or ½ dried red
  chilli, crumbled, or chopped
  parsley
salt and freshly ground black pepper

1. Heat the oil in a large frying pan over a high heat, then add the pork and cut, turning frequently, until browned.

2. Meanwhile, slice the garlic and thinly slice the red pepper. Add to the pan, lower the heat and cook for a further 10 minutes or so until the pepper and pork are cooked. Add the wine towards the end of cooking; most of it should evaporate by the time the dish is ready.

3. Add the chilli flakes, chilli or parsley and seasoning. Heat together briefly, then serve.

PORK (OR VEAL) WITH WHITE WINE

•

—— SERVES 4 ——

Traditionally veal is cooked in this way to add more 'oomph' to the rather bland meat. I use pork as any veal chops are difficult to get, and those from calves reared humanely are even more difficult to find. Most pork now on sale is also fairly tasteless and it, too, benefits from the wine and sage treatment.

3 tablespoons olive oil
4 pork steaks, each weighing about
  150g (5oz)
10 sage leaves

about 150ml ($\frac{1}{4}$ pint) medium-bodied
  dry white wine
salt and freshly ground black pepper

1. Heat the oil in a large heavy frying pan, then add the pork and cook until brown on both sides. Add the sage leaves towards the end.

2. Stir the wine into the pan as best you can, and bring to the boil. Lower the heat and continue to cook the pork for about 10–15 minutes, turning the steaks over halfway through.

3. Transfer the pork to warm plates. If necessary, boil the remaining wine so that it is not too thin. Season, pour over the pork and serve.

BREADCRUMBED VEAL ESCALOPES WITH BASIL AND PARMESAN CHEESE

•

—— SERVES 2 ——

THIS is an adaptation of veal Milanese; to give the classic dish more flavour I have added Parmesan cheese to the breadcrumbs and basil to the egg, and I squeeze lemon juice over the veal before cooking. Sometimes I also deglaze the pan with lemon juice. Creamed potatoes and fennel or courgettes are good accompaniments.

½ lemon, halved
4 veal escalopes, each weighing about 50g (2oz)
3 basil leaves, finely shredded
1 egg
2 tablespoons freshly grated Parmesan cheese

25g (1oz) plus 1 tablespoon dry breadcrumbs
olive oil and butter for frying
salt and freshly ground black pepper
lemon wedges to serve

1. Squeeze lemon juice over the veal. Using a fork, beat the basil and salt into the egg. Mix the Parmesan and black pepper into the breadcrumbs.

2. Dip each veal escalope in the egg to coat lightly on both sides, then turn in the breadcrumbs. Pat the breadcrumbs lightly in place, then shake off the excess.

3. Heat a little oil and butter in a large, heavy frying pan over a moderately high heat. Add the veal in a single layer and cook until brown on one side. Turn the veal over and cook until just golden on the other.

4. Drain the veal on paper towels. Serve with lemon wedges.

GRILLED LAMB CUTLETS WITH ROSEMARY

•

To ALLOW the lamb to be imbued with the flavour of the garlic, oil and lemon juice, in typical Italian fashion, make Step 1 the first thing you do when you prepare the meal.

1 clove garlic
3 tablespoons virgin olive oil, plus
  extra for brushing
1 tablespoon lemon juice

2 lamb chump chops, about 2.5cm
  (1 inch) thick
a few sprigs of rosemary
salt and freshly ground black pepper

1. Finely crush the garlic with a pinch of salt, then mix with the oil, lemon juice and pepper. Brush over the lamb; leave for 30–60 minutes if possible, or at least while the grill is heating.

2. Preheat the grill. Lay the rosemary sprigs on the grill rack and put the chops on top. Grill for 1 minute on each side, brushing the chops with oil as they are turned. Turn the grill down slightly and cook the lamb for 4 minutes without turning.

3. Season with salt and serve.

LAMB WITH QUICK PEPERONATA

•

—— SERVES 4 ——

PEPERONATA, also spelled *peberonata*, is sometimes referred to as the Italian version of French ratatouille, but peperonata does not contain courgettes or aubergines, just onions, tomatoes and peppers. In the traditional recipe the vegetables are cooked slowly until softened and their flavours meld together, but here they are cooked quickly so that they retain their shape and the individual flavours remain distinct. You can replace some of the red and/or yellow peppers with green pepper if you like. The quick peperonata also goes well with grilled beef steaks or pork chops or steaks.

1 tablespoon olive oil, plus extra for brushing
1 small onion, quite finely chopped
1 clove garlic, chopped
1 red pepper
1 yellow pepper
1 well-flavoured tomato

a pinch of chopped rosemary
115ml (4fl oz) vegetable stock
1 teaspoon sun-dried tomato paste
4 lamb steaks, each weighing 175–225g (6–8oz)
salt and freshly ground black pepper

1. Preheat the grill. Heat the oil in a frying pan, add the onion and garlic and cook until they are soft and transparent; do not allow them to colour.

2. Meanwhile, chop the peppers and seed and chop the tomatoes.

3. Add the peppers to the pan containing the onion and cook for about 1 minute. Stir in the tomato and rosemary. After a few seconds add the stock and tomato paste. Boil until the peppers have softened but still retain some bite.

4. While the peperonata is cooking, season one side of each lamb steak with pepper and brush with olive oil. Grill the lamb for about 4 minutes depending on thickness until brown and cooked to your liking. Season the second side of each steak and brush with oil when turning the lamb over.

5. Season the peperonata and serve with the lamb.

LAMB CUTLETS GRILLED WITH HERBS

•

You can make this for four people by doubling the ingredients, providing you can fit all the cutlets beneath the grill – remember that most grills are cooler around the edges than in the centre so you will have to reposition the cutlets during cooking. To add a light garlic flavour, rub the cutlets with a halved garlic clove before seasoning them with the pepper.

20g (¾oz) butter, chopped
1 tablespoon virgin olive oil
6 lamb cutlets, each weighing about
   115g (4oz)

chopped leaves from a small handful
   of mixed herbs such as mint,
   marjoram, basil, parsley, thyme
   and rosemary
salt and freshly ground black pepper

1. Preheat the grill. Heat the butter and oil in a small saucepan.

2. Season the lamb cutlets with pepper and brush both sides with the oil and butter mixture. Place on the grill rack and sprinkle the tops of the cutlets with half of the herbs. Grill for 2–3 minutes, depending on how well you like lamb to be cooked.

3. Turn the cutlets over, brush with the juices from the grill pan and sprinkle with the remaining herbs. Grill for a further 2–3 minutes.

4. Transfer to warm plates, brush with the grill pan juices and sprinkle with salt.

STEAK WITH TOMATOES AND OLIVES

•

—— SERVES 4 ——

Aim for 12 slices of steak; if you buy the meat from a butcher he should slice it for you. If you slice the meat yourself, you will find it easier if it is really cold, and, of course, if your knife is very sharp. Alternatively, you could use minute steaks; cook them for about 1–2 minutes a side.

3 tablespoons olive oil, plus extra for brushing
1 small onion, finely chopped
2 cloves garlic
2 well-flavoured beefsteak tomatoes
a small handful of pitted black olives

a pinch of dried oregano
450g (1lb) frying or grilling steak, thinly sliced
salt and freshly ground black pepper
chopped parsley to serve

1. Heat the oil in a frying pan, add the onion and cook until softened and lightly coloured.

2. Meanwhile, chop the garlic and add to the onion towards the end of cooking.

3. Seed and chop the tomatoes. Halve or quarter the olives. Add the tomatoes and olives to the onion with the oregano and pepper and simmer for about 15 minutes.

4. While the sauce is cooking, heat another frying pan, brush with oil, then quickly fry the beef slices just long enough to brown them.

5. Season the meat and slip the slices into the sauce. Turn them over, baste a few times with the sauce, then serve sprinkled with chopped parsley.

STEAK WITH GARLIC AND HERBS

•

—— SERVES 4 ——

THIS is an ideal treatment for good-quality steaks, although it does not qualify for the title *Fiorentenina*. This famous Tuscan dish is made from charcoal-grilled thick T-bone steaks from Tuscan-reared Val di Chiana cattle, which have a very special and particular quality, flavour and texture.

4 sirloin steaks, each weighing about 175g (6oz)
2 cloves garlic, halved
virgin olive oil
about 2 tablespoons chopped mixed herbs such as parsley, thyme, marjoram and basil

salt and freshly ground black pepper
4 lemon wedges to serve

1. Preheat the grill. Rub the steaks thoroughly with the cut sides of the garlic and brush with the oil. Season with pepper.

2. Grill the steaks for about 2–4 minutes a side, according to taste.

3. Sprinkle with the herbs and salt and serve accompanied by lemon wedges.

STEAK PIZZAIOLA

•

—— SERVES 4 ——

O REGANO is the traditional herb to use for this southern Italian dish, but if it is not available replace it with 3 tablespoons of chopped parsley. Depending on time and preference, the tomatoes can be peeled.

3 tablespoons olive oil
4 thin sirloin or rump steaks, each
  weighing 150–175g (5–6oz)
2 cloves garlic
550g (1¼lb) well-flavoured tomatoes

2 sprigs of oregano or ¼ teaspoon
  dried oregano
3 tablespoons chopped basil
salt and freshly ground black pepper

1. Heat the oil in a frying pan, add the steaks and fry over a high heat for about 2 minutes a side.

2. Meanwhile, crush the garlic and chop the tomatoes. Add the garlic to the frying pan, fry until fragrant, then add the tomatoes, oregano, basil and seasoning. Cook for 3–5 minutes until the tomatoes have softened and released their juices and these have reduced slightly.

SAUSAGES WITH POLENTA

•

—— SERVES 4 ——

POLENTA makes an enticingly savoury, warming and rustic 'porridge' that is a perfect accompaniment to hearty casseroles, or the basis of a range of tasty dishes. Traditional polenta takes a while to cook, and must be stirred. However, quick-cook polenta is now available in a number of supermarkets and, although it does not have the same character as its traditional brother, it is worth keeping in the store cupboard for occasions when you want something that is quick to make and both satisfying and interesting to eat.

2 tablespoons olive oil
450g (1lb) spicy fresh Italian
   sausages, cut into 7.5cm (3 inch)
   lengths
115g (4oz) sliced pancetta or thick-
   cut bacon, cut into strips
1 small onion
225–300g (8–10oz) wild or brown
   cap mushrooms

$1\frac{1}{2}$ well-flavoured beefsteak
   tomatoes
300g (10oz) quick-cook polenta
salt and freshly ground black pepper
shredded basil or chopped parsley
   to garnish
freshly grated Parmesan cheese to
   serve

1. Heat the oil in a large frying pan, then add the sausages and pancetta or bacon and fry until the sausages are brown and the fat is beginning to run from the pancetta or bacon. Remove and reserve.

2. While the sausages are cooking, finely chop the onion and add to the pan to join the sausages and pancetta or bacon as they cook.

3. Chop the mushrooms; seed and chop the tomatoes.

4. When you have removed the sausages and pancetta or bacon, add the mushrooms to the pan and cook for 2–3 minutes before adding the tomatoes. Return the sausages and pancetta or bacon to the pan and cook for about 15 minutes.

5. Meanwhile, cook the polenta according to the directions on the pack, then pour into a warm, large dish and make a depression in the centre.

6. Season the sauce surrounding the sausages and pour, with the sausages, on to the polenta. Garnish with shredded basil or chopped parsley and serve with freshly grated Parmesan.

ZAMPONE ON BRAISED LENTILS

•

SERVES 4

Tʜɪs makes a welcoming country-style winter dish. Zampone is a boned pig's trotter filled with minced pork, spices or herbs, and some skin, which gives it a wonderful silky texture. Traditionally, it requires about 2 hours simmering, but nowadays vacuum-packed zampone can be bought from Italian food shops and is ready to eat in 20 minutes.

2 tablespoons olive oil
1 small onion, chopped
1 clove garlic
1 vacuum-packed zampone,
  weighing about 600g (1lb 6oz)

300g (10oz) brown lentils
bouquet garni
1 × 400g (14oz) can chopped
  tomatoes
salt and freshly ground black pepper

1. Pour enough water to cover the zampone into a wide saucepan or a frying pan that is large and deep enough to hold the zampone. Bring to the boil. Alternatively, bring the water to the boil in an electric kettle.

2. Meanwhile, heat the oil in a saucepan, add the onion and fry for 2–3 minutes while you crush and chop the garlic. Add the garlic to the onion and continue to cook for 2–3 minutes.

3. When the water for the zampone comes to the boil, add the zampone, cover and simmer for 15–20 minutes or according to the directions on the pack.

4. Stir the lentils, bouquet garni and tomatoes into the pan with the onion and add enough water to just cover them. Bring to the boil, then simmer for 15–20 minutes until the lentils are tender. Add more water only if necessary; the lentils should not need draining at the end of cooking. Season before serving.

5. Drain the zampone, cut into slices and serve with the lentils.

CHAPTER SIX

•

Desserts

F<small>RESH</small> fruit has for a long time been a favourite way of ending a meal in Italy – which is hardly surprising when you think of the luscious, seasonal, flavour-packed produce Italians have on their doorsteps. The fruit is often eaten as it comes, but can easily be made into more special desserts by, for example, mixing it with ricotta and mascarpone cheeses. Desserts like these will be particularly satisfying if you have only had a light meal.

Plain cheese and fruit is also a popular way of ending a meal. Try some glowing, fresh Parmesan with ripe pears, perhaps adding some walnuts in their shells in autumn. Pears also go well with creamy Gorgonzola, while plump, juicy black grapes are a good partner for taleggio; buy more of this than you think you will need as the rind should be discarded.

Or you could simply finish your meal with a small glass of lusciously sweet *vin santo* into which you dip crisp, dry almonds.

Peaches Stuffed with Amaretti and Ricotta

•

—— SERVES 4 ——

STUFFED peaches is one dish that is sure to come to mind when you think of Italian desserts, so here is a good, quick recipe.

6 amaretti biscuits
50g (2oz) ricotta cheese

4 ripe well-flavoured peaches
sugar for sprinkling

1. Preheat the grill. Leave the amaretti in their wrappers and crush them with a rolling pin.

2. Beat the crushed amaretti into the ricotta cheese.

3. Cut the peaches in half and remove the stones. Fill the cavities with the ricotta mixture. Sprinkle with a little sugar and grill for 5–7 minutes until browned. Serve warm.

REALLY QUICK STUFFED PEACHES

•

—— SERVES 4 ——

RIPE white peaches are particularly good for this ultra-quick dessert. If you do not have any amaretti biscuits you can serve the dessert as it is; or sprinkle the cheese with icing or brown sugar, depending on whether you want the smooth, sweet effect of icing sugar or the crunch of brown sugar. Alternatively, you could sieve some fresh raspberries over the top.

4 well-flavoured ripe peaches; white are particularly good

4–6 heaped tablespoons chilled mascarpone cheese

3–4 amaretti biscuits

1. Halve the peaches and remove the stones. Put two peach halves on each of 4 plates and spoon the cheese into the cavities left by the stones.

2. Crush the amaretti biscuits in their wrappers, using a rolling pin, then sprinkle them over the peaches and serve.

STRAWBERRIES IN RED WINE

•

—— SERVES 4 ——

A NUMBER of fruits go well with red wine, but strawberries are probably the best example.

450g (1lb) ripe strawberries   4 glasses red wine
caster sugar

Divide the strawberries between 4 individual serving dishes, sprinkle them with a little caster sugar then pour the wine over them.

Alternatively serve a bowl of strawberries, a bowl of sugar and 4 glasses of wine and leave everyone to pop their own berries into their wine. Sugar can be added to taste and the fruit scooped out with a spoon.

STRAWBERRIES WITH BALSAMIC VINEGAR

•

—— SERVES 4 ——

A LTHOUGH this has become quite a trendy dessert, sprinkling rich balsamic vinegar over strawberries to highlight their flavour has been done in Modena, the home of balsamic vinegar, for a long time.

450g (1lb) ripe strawberries   caster sugar
3–4 tablespoons balsamic vinegar

1. Put the strawberries into a serving bowl, or 4 individual bowls, and gently stir in the vinegar. Leave for about 10 minutes.

2. Mix in caster sugar to taste, and serve.

STRAWBERRY CRUSH WITH MASCARPONE AND RICOTTA

•

—— SERVES 4 ——

Lovers of very rich desserts may be happy to use just mascarpone, but I prefer to counteract its richness with ricotta, varying the proportions of the cheese according to how light I want the dessert to be. Depending on the strawberries and your taste, you might like to add some orange juice or balsamic vinegar, and/or a little sugar when crushing the strawberries. I like to make the Crush before preparing the rest of the meal so that it can be left to 'mature' for a while.

450g (1lb) strawberries　　　　　*175g (6oz) mascarpone cheese*
75g (3oz) ricotta cheese　　　　　*amaretti biscuits to serve*

1. Reserve some of the strawberries for decoration and crush the remainder in a bowl, using a fork.

2. Sieve in the ricotta cheese, then add the mascarpone cheese and mix all the ingredients together; take care not to break up the strawberries any further. Leave for as long as possible before serving.

3. Decorate with the reserved strawberries and serve with amaretti biscuits.

Italian Raspberry Layer

•

I F YOU can, make this dessert when you start to prepare the meal so that it can be chilled and the flavour has time to develop. However, this is not obligatory and you will still enjoy it if it is made later. Icing sugar will dissolve more quickly than caster sugar.

175g (6oz) ricotta cheese
75g (3oz) mascarpone cheese
about 2 tablespoons icing or caster
  sugar to taste

rose water to taste
about 450g (1lb) raspberries
amaretti biscuits to serve

1. Sieve the ricotta cheese or beat it in a bowl. Stir in the mascarpone cheese, icing or caster sugar and rose water to taste.

2. Reserve some of the raspberries for decoration. Place alternate spoonfuls of the cheese mixture and the remaining raspberries in individual dishes or a large dish. Chill for up to 30 minutes if possible, then decorate with the reserved raspberries and serve with amaretti biscuits.

GLAZED MASCARPONE CHEESE ON SUMMER BERRIES

•

——— SERVES 4 ———

WITH its luscious topping of crisp-crusted, thick-velvet mascarpone cheese over fragrant, fresh raspberries, this dessert makes a fitting end to a special meal. Or you can make it simply because you feel like indulging yourself. Well-flavoured sun-ripened strawberries or plump blackberries can be used instead of, or with, raspberries.

250g (9oz) fresh raspberries
200g (7oz) mascarpone cheese

about 75g (3oz) caster sugar

1. Preheat the grill to very hot.

2. Put the raspberries in a heatproof dish and spoon the mascarpone cheese over the top. Sprinkle with the sugar and grill for 2–3 minutes until the sugar has caramelised.

ICE CREAM WITH ESPRESSO

•

—— SERVES 4 ——

THE best way to get the maximum contrast between hot, bitter coffee and warm-flavoured but cold, creamy ice cream – without the ice cream melting too much – is to transfer the ice cream to the refrigerator before you start preparing the meal. Leave it there for about 15 minutes so that it is soft enough to scoop, then return the scoops to the freezer to harden again.

8 scoops of dairy vanilla ice cream *crisp biscuits to serve*
4 espresso cups of freshly made
  espresso coffee

Put the ice cream scoops into 4 cold, individual dishes. Pour the coffee over them and serve immediately with crisp biscuits.

CAPPUCINO CREAMS

•

─── SERVES 4 ───

I ASSEMBLE this quick, no-cook dessert before I start to prepare the rest of the meal, if not earlier, as the flavour improves if it has time to mellow. If liked, about 50g (2oz) mascarpone cheese can be substituted for the same amount of ricotta.

2 tablespoons rum or brandy
1–2 tablespoons espresso-grind
  coffee
$\frac{1}{2}$–1 tablespoon icing sugar

250–300g (9–10oz) ricotta cheese
grated bitter chocolate to decorate

1. Stir the rum or brandy, coffee and icing sugar into the ricotta cheese, then beat well.

2. Divide the coffee mixture between 4 individual dishes or glasses and decorate generously with chocolate. Chill for up to 2 hours if possible.

PANETTONE WITH MASCARPONE CHEESE
•

SERVES 4

PANETTONE is a buttery, light, Milanese sweet bread that used to be eaten only in Lombardy, at Christmas, but it is now available throughout Italy, and in Britain, all year. Traditionally it is studded just with dried fruits but some modern versions also include pieces of chocolate; it is this type that I like to use for this dessert. If you have been cooking in the oven you can warm the panettone in it for about 10 minutes instead of using the grill.

4 slices of panettone

4 heaped tablespoons mascarpone cheese

1. Preheat the grill.

2. Put the slices of panettone under the grill until they are warmed through and lightly toasted.

3. Transfer the panettone to warm plates and serve the mascarpone separately – when it is spooned on to the panettone it melts voluptuously into it.

Menus

Rocket, Tomato and Mozzarella Salad
*
Chicken with Savoury Basil Sauce
Sautéed Red Peppers
*
Italian Raspberry Layer

Spinach Soup
*

Grilled Lamb Cutlets with Rosemary
Glazed Leeks with Parmesan Cheese
*

Strawberries with Balsamic Vinegar

Eggs with Tuna Sauce
*

Pasta with Broccoli and Gorgonzola Cheese
*

Stuffed Peaches

Bagna Cauda
*

Fish with Polenta Crust and Basil and
Olive Vinaigrette
Simple Green Salad
*

Ice Cream with Espresso

Grilled Artichoke Salad

*

Steak with Tomatoes and Olives

*

Really Quick Stuffed Peaches

Italian Stuffed Mushrooms

*

Fish with Courgettes
Herb-Topped Tomatoes (cooked in the oven)

*

Glazed Mascarpone Cheese on Summer Berries

Index